ARE YOU BEING BULLIED?

Kathleen Winkler

SHOUTING

SHAMING

TORMENT

CYBERBULLYING

NAME CALLING

Enslow Publishers, Inc.
40 Industrial Road
Box 398
Berkeley Heights, NJ 07922
USA
http://www.enslow.com

Library of Congress Cataloging-in-Publication Data
Winkler, Kathleen.
  Are you being bullied? : how to deal with taunting, teasing, and tormenting / Kathleen Winkler.
     pages cm. — (Got issues?)
  Includes bibliographical references and index.
  ISBN 978-0-7660-5953-5
  1. Bullying—Juvenile literature. 2. Bullying in schools—Juvenile literature. 3. Aggressiveness in
  adolescence—Juvenile literature. I. Title.
  BF637.B85W557 2014 302.34'3—dc23

                                        2013049842

Future Editions:
Paperback ISBN: 978-0-7660-5954-2   Single-User PDF ISBN: 978-0-7660-5956-6
EPUB ISBN: 978-0-7660-5955-9   Multi-User PDF ISBN: 978-0-7660-5957-3

Printed in the United States of America
062014 Lake Book Manufacturing, Inc., Melrose Park, IL
10 9 8 7 6 5 4 3 2 1

To Our Readers: We have done our best to make sure all Internet Addresses in this book were active and
appropriate when we went to press. However, the author and the publisher have no control over and assume
no liability for the material available on those Internet sites or on other Web sites they may link to. Any
comments or suggestions can be sent by e-mail to comments@enslow.com or to the address on the back
cover.

♻ Enslow Publishers, Inc., is committed to printing our books on recycled paper. The paper in every book
contains 10% to 30% post-consumer waste (PCW). The cover board on the outside of each book contains
100% PCW. Our goal is to do our part to help young people and the environment too!

Illustration Credits: AP Images/Chris Schneider, p. 29; Shutterstock.com (©Creatista, p. 76; ©Dave
Wetzel, p. 40; ©ejwhite, p. 21; ©Gemenacom, p. 17; ©Jason Stitt, p. 45; ©jaymast, p. 31; ©littleny, p. 36;
©Mandy Godbehear, p. 5; ©Milkovasa, p. 48; ©Monkey Business Images, pp. 51, 63; ©oliveromg, pp. 1,
42; ©Patricia Marks, 25; ©Rob Marmion, p. 67; ©zhu difeng, p. 60); ©Thinkstock (Christopher Futcher,
p. 74; Hemera Technologies, p. 70; Jupiterimages, p. 56; Sorin Alb, p. 11; Thinkstock Images, p. 13;
VBStock, pp. 7, 80).

Cover Illustration: Shutterstock.com/©oliveromg

Contents

One Teen's Story

"Chandra" (not her real name) knows what it is like to be bullied. Sixth and seventh grade were miserable for her because she was a target.

Chandra also knows what it is like to bully. In eighth grade, when she was "top of the heap," she turned into a bully herself, targeting others. She found that being a bully did not make her feel any happier than being the victim.

Chandra was being bullied and bullying at school. It started in early grade school when Chandra became the student everyone else in the class liked to pick on. In many cases a child is bullied because he or she is shy and will not talk back. That does not seem to be the case with Chandra. She has always been an outspoken person, even as a small child, she says. She is not sure exactly why she was chosen to be picked on, although she has some guesses. Looking back, Chandra, now a college student, thinks the root of her problem getting along in grade school was her early development and her intelligence. She says:

> I went through puberty early for one thing, and I was always one of the smarter kids in the class. I was in the gifted and talented program; I was always outspoken in class and really interested in learning. I wasn't ashamed of participating, and that made me stand out. Those things combined really caused people to not like me—anyone who stands out in middle school, who is not blending in, is the object of ridicule.

Whatever the reason, by the time she reached sixth grade, it seemed that everyone in her class and the classes above her had ganged up to make her life miserable.

"I remember that the kids really made fun of me," she recalls, pain still in her voice.

She says:

> One day I had a tube of lip balm that I was putting on a cold sore during class. The teacher said, "Why are you putting that on in class?" I said, "Because I have a cold sore." He said, "Isn't a cold sore herpes? Does that mean you have herpes?" I laughed nervously and tried to let it pass, but the kids called me "herpes" for months.

Both boys and girls (and, some might say, that teacher) were guilty of the bullying, but they went about it in different ways. Chandra says:

> Boys teased me individually or maybe in twos, but with girls it was large groups that would make fun of me. A lot of times the girls would play tricks on me. Boys would laugh and point and say, "You're fat," but the girls would play jokes like telling me boys liked me when they really didn't. Or they would try to get me to say stupid things so they could laugh at me. They would point out over and over that I was not friends with them. I was an outspoken kid so most times I would try to come up with comebacks to their

Bullying can include teasing, name-calling, and physical attacks such as hitting and shoving.

teasing, but that was pretty much in vain since all the kids were bullying me together.

When smart comebacks did not work, Chandra decided to try much harder to get along with the other kids. "I started to try really hard to make friends with the bullies' friends, and I tried to fit in more with them, hoping they wouldn't think I was such a big loser," she says. "For a while it sort of worked and I started getting along with more kids, but the bullying in middle school never really ended."

As time moved on, the worst kids moved on to high school. "Once I was in eighth grade, it started changing, getting better," she says. "The kids who were older than me, who had been taunting me, were in high school by then."

However, "better" is a relative term. Chandra says:

> In some ways it was better, but in some ways it got worse. In eighth grade I started becoming—well, I wouldn't say introverted because I've always been outgoing—but I started becoming hateful about things. I was just really negative about everything. I had internalized a lot of things the other kids had said to me. I started thinking that since I was in eighth grade, I could start taking things out on other people.

The bullied became the bully.

> Someone I had gone to grade school with told me recently that I spit in his face and threw him up against the wall. I don't remember it, but apparently I did that. I got in trouble for roughing up a kid on the bus—I wouldn't call it beating him up, but I was physically pushing him around. I started doing that to younger kids who would make me mad for no reason. I was never as cruel as people had been to me, but I sure did my best to get my anger out!

Unfortunately, being a bully brought on anger and a desire for revenge in the other kids. Chandra says:

> When I started acting angry and brooding, a new wave of teasing started. Kids my age started calling me names and there were a lot of rumors about me doing drugs and having sex, which weren't true. There were a lot of fat jokes, and people constantly called me a lesbian or a slut. Sometimes I was so angry about it I just claimed the rumors and said, "Yeah, they're true." People accusing me of drugs and sex sort of drove me to those areas quicker. I already had the stigma, people were already thinking I was this druggy, or this slut, so I sort of went in that direction. I never went way downhill or anything. But I was definitely dabbling a bit before everybody else because I'd already had all this ridicule from kids about it.

When eighth grade finally ended, Chandra told her parents that she just could not handle those kids anymore and asked if she could go to a different school. Her parents agreed, and Chandra went to a private high school. She says:

> That was a lot better. Although I don't recommend running from your problems, it really solved mine. Nobody knew me at that school and I definitely started over. Nothing like that started up again. My grades went up and things got a lot better in general. The desire to fight and bully went away with maturity—in ninth grade I was at the bottom of the chain again. I didn't have anyone to bully and I was growing out of it anyway. My high school years were really happy.

Chandra finds it hard to give advice to kids who might be going through the same thing she did because some things that happened to her seem contradictory. But she is willing to say:

> It's hard to know what to do—I was an outspoken kid and I still got trampled on. There are kids out there who are much more shy than I was and they are being crushed. It's very hard to get kids to stop teasing.
>
> I would recommend keeping your relationships, like your family and the friends you do have, close and tight. They will help you to know who you really are and to get through the teasing. Make friends who are willing to stand up for you. You need somebody on your side, you need that net to fall on.

Some adults can sometimes be a help, Chandra says:

> Ideally, you should have some adults on your side too. I don't regret not talking to some of my teachers more about it because there's only so much they can do, and you really do get made fun of if you go to the teachers. That's the "telling" thing. Some of my teachers seemed to have the attitude that boys will be boys and the girls are harmless. That never helped me.

Schools are now doing more about bullying, however, and Chandra's experience might be quite different today.

School activities can also be a good thing, she says. "I was in forensics and band and that really helped to get my mind off the teasing," she says. "I do recommend getting involved."

Chandra still sometimes sees or hears from some of the kids she went to grade school with. She still holds anger toward them. She says:

> There was one boy who spread horrible lies about things that didn't happen between us. He called me in high school, three years after the fact, and apologized. He said he was sorry he ruined my reputation. I wasn't sure if he was sincere or not—but then I heard a bunch of people burst out laughing in the background. I just hung up. There are two people from my grade school going to college with me; they once called at 1:00 in the morning. I said, "I don't want to talk to you right now." The one guy said, "Gee, you are just as [mean] as you were in grade school." I thought, "What is wrong with you?" and I said, "Leave me alone, I don't want to talk to you ever again." I hung up on him too. I guess some people never grow out of it.

> But I know who I am now, so it's a lot less unsettling than it was at a time when I really didn't know who I was. I'm not bothered by the bullying now, but I think it definitely changed the way I see things. My brother is sixteen, and if I overhear him calling someone a slut, I really jump in and say, "Wait a minute—why are you saying something like that?" It's really made me not so quick to put labels on people.[1]

> Unfortunately, Chandra's experience with bullying is not unusual. It happens to thousands of kids, boys and girls, every day in schools all around the world. In this book we will try to answer some questions. Who does it and why? Who are the victims and why do they take it? What are the effects on bullies and victims? What are schools doing about it? What should both bullies and victims do to stop the cycle of violence?

2

Bullying: What Is It? Who Does It?

With the increase in shootings in recent years in schools and public places, half the world seems to be saying, "Bullying has gotten so much worse," while the other half is saying, "There have always been bullies; we just take it more seriously now."

Who is right? Probably both. While people have always paid attention to bullying, horrific events beginning in 1999 with Colorado's Columbine High School (in which two troubled students, thought to have been bullied, shot and killed twelve of their classmates and one teacher) helped focus the nation's attention on the problem. There has been much serious research since, and researchers are looking at some older studies, done before Columbine, with a fresh eye.

What Is Bullying?

One of the problems in doing research on bullying is defining exactly what the word means. Does bullying mean only hitting, shoving, or stomping on someone? Does it include calling names or teasing someone about a big nose? Does it include shutting someone out of a social group? Does it include racial slurs or degrading remarks about someone's sexuality? Does it only take place in person, face to face, or can it include things written to or about someone online?

This is the most often used definition: Bullying is any kind of ongoing physical or verbal mistreatment, done with the intent to harm, where there is an imbalance of power between bully and victim. It usually, but not always, means a bigger, older child picking on a smaller or weaker one, or a more popular child picking on a less popular one.

In some ways, bullying is like a game of "one-upmanship;" an attempt to win while the other person loses. Usually the victim is very upset (unlike normal childhood teasing). The bully often does not see his or her actions as being out of line.[1] Sometimes, unfortunately, the line between "just teasing" and bullying can seem very hazy. Both victims and bullies can be unaware of the difference.

Bullying behaviors can be direct: teasing, taunting, threatening, hitting, or stealing the victim's belongings. They can also be indirect: spreading rumors, or causing a student to be socially isolated by excluding him or her. In general, boys engage in direct bullying more often, while girls are more likely to use indirect bullying. Although there are certainly exceptions.[2] Some research has found that direct bullying behavior goes up during the elementary school years, peaks in middle school, and goes down in high school.[3]

How Often Does It Happen?

Bullying is not something that can be measured scientifically like counting the number of peas in a pod or calculating the percentage of sugar in soft drinks. Research studies, therefore, do not come up

Some people recommend getting involved in school activities, such as musical groups, to help combat teasing.

with the same numbers. In fact, some have produced contradictory numbers. But they all agree there is a lot of bullying going on. Here is what some research studies have found, complete with differences in conclusions:

- A survey of fifteen thousand U.S. schoolchildren by the National Institute of Child Health and Human Development found that 29 percent of them have been involved in bullying during the current school term, either as bullies or victims.[4]

- An online survey of three thousand teenagers conducted by Secret antiperspirant and seventeen.com found that half had experienced physical threats in the past year. Of that half, 44 percent were girls and 56 percent were boys.[5] This, it should be noted, is not a scientifically valid survey (self-reported Internet surveys never are), but it gives a picture of what some teens are thinking.

- The National Association of School Psychologists says that about one in seven schoolchildren, about 5 million kids, has been either a bully or a victim.[6]

- Bullying seems to be common in rural areas. One study showed that in the rural American Midwest, 90 percent of middle school students and 66 percent of high school students reported having been bullied.[7]

- A survey by the U.S. Centers for Disease Control and Prevention said that ten thousand children stayed home from school at least once a month because they feared bullies. Half of the children surveyed said that they were bullied once a week.[8]

- A 1999 poll by *ABC News* and the *Washington Post* said that four in ten high school students believe they have classmates who feel troubled enough to carry out a Columbine-style massacre. One in five claims to know a fellow student who has brought a gun to school.[9]

Who Are the Bullies?

Everyone has a mental image of a bully as a big, rough-looking guy lurking in a corner of the schoolyard, waiting for his next victim to walk by. Research shows that, while that is a picture of some bullies, it is not true of all of them.

We will look more closely in the next chapter at why kids bully and why victims take it. For now, there are some myths about bullies that need to be debunked.

One is that only boys are bullies. "Statistics show that boys are more likely than girls to engage in . . . physical violence," says psychologist Peter Sheras, in his book about bullying. "Female bullies commonly act by spreading rumors, teasing, ostracizing, and otherwise causing emotional torment."[10]

Another myth says that bullies are social outcasts. This is not always true either, especially in younger children. The bully may be quite popular. "Bullies have been shown in a number of studies to enjoy an average or above-average level of popularity," Dr. Sheras says.[11]

Who Gets Bullied?

While many kids who are picked on seem to be "lame" or "nerds" or are different in some way, other victims do not fit those categories at all.

Some studies have suggested that until about age seven, bullies pick on anyone. After that, they pick out specific kids to bully. One researcher, Dr. Hara Marano, calls them "whipping boys" because kids seem to use them as their targets over and over.[12]

A 1991 survey done at Ohio University said that junior and senior high school students identify a victim as "someone who does not fit in, has a different religion, wears unique or unusual clothes, has a physical weakness or is different in appearance."[13] However, Dr. Sheras writes, such factors alone do not mean that a student will be picked on. The victim usually has other characteristics including having few friends and low self-esteem.[14]

Kids who are picked on usually give in to bullies' demands quickly and easily. They may act submissive even before they are picked on. They do not know how to approach other kids, how to make conversation, or how to make friends.[15]

"No one likes a bully, but no one likes a victim either," Dr. Marano says."[16]

Bullies and victims may seem to be locked into a strange relationship, acting out the roles over and over and causing much emotional pain.

Why Do Bullies Do It and Why Do Victims Take It?

The school-yard world is populated by both bullies and victims. Someone watching them from outside the playground fence might wonder why kids are so mean to each other. Why do some kids swagger around like they own the world? Why do other kids shrink in fear or cry when they are tormented?

Bullying was not on the "radar screen" for many years. Some researchers were looking at it as long ago as the early 1980s, but the media did not cover it and it was not really part of people's thinking. Then came some school shootings that were heavily covered by the media, and interest stepped up, as did research funds. Bullying has gone on for all of human history, social scientists thought, and it was time to find out why. Learning more about the reasons kids bully would help to find ways to make it less common.

Researchers began to study why it is that some kids bully others and why other kids are so often the victims. What they learned tells us a lot about both bullies and their victims.

Bullies: Why They Do It

Brent was certainly not the type of boy anyone would suspect of being a bully, writes Peter Sheras, a psychologist who has worked with both bullies and victims. Brent's older brothers had been successful and popular in high school and were now in college. Brent was good-looking and had the "right" clothes and lots of friends.

When a student told the vice principal that Brent had beaten him up on the soccer field after school, she could hardly believe it. But then other kids began to report being mistreated by Brent, and finally he had a fight in public. Brent, it turned out, had been picked on by his brothers all through his childhood. His parents did not pay any attention. The older brothers had also been bullies in high school. Brent's friends admitted they were afraid of him rather than liking him.[1]

In another case of bullying, a victim named John had been bullied in high school. Twenty years later, he found the name and e-mail address of one of the bullies on the Internet and sent him an e-mail. The resulting e-mail exchange showed some interesting things about the bully.

"I, too, was harassed in high school," the former bully wrote back to John. He apologized for his part in the bullying but said it really had nothing to do with John personally. The former bully said he had a lot of confusion and frustration about his own "issues of anger" at losing his father.[2]

If these two stories tell us anything, it is that bullies can be very different and have very different reasons for their bullying.

Dr. Bruce Nerenberg, a psychologist who works with teenagers in his private practice, says that reasons for bullying vary greatly. The following are some of the reasons most commonly thought to motivate bullies.

Power. "A lot of bullying has to do with the struggle for control or power," Dr. Nerenberg says. "If you can gain control over others, or cause them to fear you, you have power. A child can mistake fear for respect."[3]

Self-esteem issues. Dr. Nerenberg has seen bullies who have low self-esteem and are trying to feel better about themselves by bullying others. But he has also seen bullies who have high self-esteem. "I'm not sure why they think they rule the world, but they do," he says.[4]

Studies show Dr. Nerenberg is right: There are some bullies who have very high self-esteem. They may not even be aware that other kids fear and dislike them. Melissa DeRosier, a psychologist at the University of North Carolina, writes, "Bullies are clueless as to how little they are liked; they are out of touch with what kids think."[5]

A study done in England showed that many bullies have a positive self-concept and self-esteem. The researchers used an anonymous survey. Rather than ask kids directly, "Are you a bully?" they used a list of statements such as "I have tried to hit or kick someone" or "I have demanded money from someone" to identify the bullies. Those in the study who were bullies scored higher in self-esteem than the children who were not. The bullies thought of themselves as being popular. "The generally positive self-concept of these young people implies that they see themselves and their behavior as acceptable, or that they are confident enough not to care," the researchers write.[6]

Having poor social skills. Part of the bully/victim puzzle is the bully's lack of social skills, says Dr. Nerenberg:

> *Kids who have poor social skills can become bullies because they don't know how to develop friendships. Bullying becomes a substitute for friendship. They don't know how to be a friend. They don't know how to get their needs for affection, attention, or friendship met in a socially good way. They think they can do it through power and domineering.*[7]

Not seeing the world as it really is. According to Dr. Hara Marano, bullies seem to have a different way of thinking from kids who do not bully. They think everyone around them has a hostile attitude toward them. "They perceive provocation where it does not exist," she writes. "Say someone bumps them and they drop a book. Bullies don't see it as an accident; they see it as a call to arms."[8]

"[Because of that view they have] a favorable attitude toward violence and the use of violence to solve problems," Marano continues. "Bullies come to believe that aggression is the best solution to conflicts." They also have a strong need to dominate, and they get satisfaction from hurting others.[9]

Lack of empathy. Bullies also seem to lack the ability to understand what other people are feeling. We call that ability empathy. "Empathy is being able to stand inside somebody's shoes and know how it feels," says Dr. Nerenberg. "There are some people who never get there."[10] Because they have never learned how painful their actions are to other kids, bullies may actually enjoy causing them pain.

Learned behavior. Part of bullying can also be learned. Bullies are not born, says Marilyn LaCourt, a family therapist. "We are born with certain temperaments, but how we use them is learned," she says. "Bullying is partly learned from other bullies. If dad is bullying mom, kids are going to see that it works and they might use the same kind of behavior to get their way."[11]

Television, movies, and video games can also figure into the picture. "I think we have desensitized ourselves to violence by seeing it in the movies," says LaCourt. "They can't shock us anymore. There is incredible violence in video games, too, and kids are playing them all the time."[12]

That opinion is also borne out by research. A study at the Center for Adolescent Studies at Indiana University found that those who reported the most bullying behavior were also most likely to report viewing high levels of TV violence. They also reported spending less time with adults.[13] Having nonviolent adults as role models may help to counteract the violence on TV.

Being abused. One study looked at a group of children at a summer day camp; some of them had been abused earlier in life,

Studies have shown that people who experienced violence in their homes are more likely to become bullies than those who have not.

some had not. The study showed that children who had been abused were significantly more likely to be bullies.[14] They often came from homes where physical punishment was used, where children were taught to strike back physically as a way to handle problems, and where their parents were not very involved and lacked warmth.[15]

Fear of being bullied. Some children join in bullying because they are afraid they might be bullied themselves if they do not. For example, a child named Brian was often bullied in early grade school. When he got to high school, he found that if he joined a gang of teens who were picking on younger kids and taking their lunch money, he would not be bullied himself. His parents were told of his behavior, but they ignored it, thinking he would grow out of it. He did not. A month before he would have graduated, he was arrested when he and his gang tied up a clerk and robbed a store.[16]

To gain social status. Some kids think that the only way to be part of the "in" crowd is to join in bullying. Middle school students especially may want to be part of the "top group" so much that they are willing to pick on others just to get the group's approval, says Dr. Sheras.[17]

There are a few other statistics that have a bearing on bullies:
- Bullying happens at about the same rate across races.
- Bullying happens most in grades six to eight.
- Bullies are more likely to smoke and use alcohol than non-bullies.
- Bullies have a harder time making friends, have poorer relationships with other students, and say they are lonely more often.
- Bullies are often defiant toward adults and are likely to break school rules.[18]

Sometimes a bully does not even realize what he or she is doing to others. One bully, looking back, wrote, "I never thought of myself as a bully, but when I think back to junior high I realize that I was incredibly cruel to one person for more than a year without even realizing what I was doing." He went on to describe how he wanted to hang out with different people other than his former best friend and how he made fun of the old friend to the new ones. He also told how

he enjoyed making the old friend cry. "It made me feel powerful ....
[Now] it makes me sad. We had such good times together, but we
never will again. I hope I have learned from my mistakes."[19]

Connie Emmons, a Florida teacher who has taught fourth grade
for many years, had a student who summed up the two sides to
many bullies. This girl was much bigger than the other children and
used that to get her way. Emmons says:

> She would knee them in the back, push them out of line, twist
> their arms or kick their legs, call them names, and threaten to
> beat them up. She always needed her own way. Once a little girl
> accidentally stepped on her foot; the bully didn't give her a chance
> to apologize. She shoved her up against the wall and twisted the
> skin on her arm until she made a black and blue mark. The child's
> mother took pictures of the bruises and threatened to go to the
> sheriff.

Emmons tried to talk to the bully's mother, but the woman
spoke no English. So she had the bully come into her classroom for
lunch and tried to get her to talk about why she treated the others
so badly. "I learned that the bully's older sister knocked her around
a lot. That's the way she was treated so she treated others the same
way," she says.

The girl was suspended from school for three days for hurting
the other little girl; that got her attention. While at home, she wrote
Emmons a letter saying she was in big trouble and wanted to learn
to be a better person.

Emmons says:

> Slowly I began making friends with her, letting her know that I
> really did like her. Whenever I could see her becoming upset I'd
> walk up close to her and say "I can help you." When someone
> did something to her accidentally I would help her to see that the
> person didn't mean it, that accidents happen.
>
> She's doing much better of late. She's calmer and seems to be
> able to handle herself better when she's upset. She told me recently

that things are going better at home, too. I was surprised to find she had a very sweet side to her.[20]

That little girl shows so many of the qualities of a typical bully. She also shows how the power of friendship can change a bully's ways.

Victims: Why They Take It

"Randi" (not her real name) is an adult who was bullied for much of her life. She says:

> *One of my earliest memories is of being with a bunch of kids and one of them running, trying to get hold of me, with a pan full of sand to put down my back. In grade school I was ignored. People called me names. It was the same in high school. In biology we were supposed to have a lab partner but no one wanted to be my partner so I just left. Whenever we went to the lab, I left—I got a D or an F in the class because I didn't do any of the work. It didn't occur to me to tell the teacher. It was like telling someone that I have brown hair—I just kind of accepted it.*

Randi is not sure exactly why she was always picked on, but looking back, she can make some guesses:

> *I think some very early messages that I got in my life made me afraid of people. I was basically terrified of the way people could be nice one minute and say nasty things the next. I think I truly believed I was bad and unworthy, that there was something wrong with me. I think other kids got that message about me.*[21]

Why are some kids repeatedly picked on while others never are? Researchers have also looked at that question.

About 7 to 10 percent of school-age children can be classified as being victims over and over, according to one study done by Dr. Judith Bernstein. "Most are extremely passive and almost never behave aggressively. They tend to be insecure, do not defend themselves, and are rejected by their peers," she writes. She also found that victims display a different pattern of behavior from

Loners, and those who have difficulty socializing, are more likely to be victims of bullies.

non-victims. They rarely approached others to play and mostly did whatever the others wanted.[22]

We will look at some of these reasons in greater depth.

Lack of social skills. Some kids are picked on because they do not know how to make friends and get along with others. They may be alone and lonely; they do not have friends they can count on to defend them. "I generally have not seen victims have good social skills any more than bullies do," says Dr. Nerenberg. "I get the sense that the victim doesn't know anything better but he or she at least knows the rules of bully and victim. It may seem too risky to break out of that role."[23]

Being a "loner" invites rejection. "Rejected children appear to be more inattentive than peers in their age group," Dr. Beverly Yahnke, a psychologist, writes. "They seem to lack enthusiasm and appear passive, frightened or shy. But some rejected children are disruptive in class and seen as troublemakers by their peers." That kind of rejection starts very early, she says.

> In the earliest elementary grades, a child may seem to exclude himself from the group and may be neglected by playmates. By the second grade, children have begun to call the shy, isolated children names. As children move from fourth through the eighth grade, the challenge of breaking into the group increases in difficulty. If you don't belong to a group by sixth grade, prospects for ever being included are dismal.[24]

Being different in some way. Kids who do not fit the "mold," who do not look right, dress right, or speak right, are often the ones picked on. "Some children are ungainly, awkward, overweight, or have some characteristic that puts them at a disadvantage given the childhood or adolescent society they live in," says Dr. Nerenberg.

> The fat child is going to be picked on for that. The overly intellectual child will be picked on for being the teacher's pet. Special education kids can be picked on; I've worked with some that are called "retards" and other names. Bullies choose their

victims because you can stand a little higher by stepping on someone else.[25]

One study found that short children, especially boys, were victimized more often than taller children. More short children claimed to have been bullied at some time in high school. Short boys were more than twice as likely as taller boys to be victims. They were also much more likely to say that the bullying upset them.[26]

A Canadian study found that 14 percent of overweight and 19 percent of extremely overweight children said they were victims of bullying, compared with 11 percent of normal weight children. They were twice as likely to be left out of social activities. (Interestingly, being very overweight also raised the risk of being a bully, especially for girls.)[27]

Having a poor self-image. Children with low self-image are at greater risk for being bullied. One researcher writes,

> *In general, children who are bullied tend to have lower self-esteem and self-confidence. They may see themselves negatively (particularly after repeated harassment and victimization) and shy away from confrontation and conflict—traits that other students may pick up on.*[28]

Having an overprotective family. "Victims [often] have close relationships with their parents and tend to come from overprotective families," Dr. Marano writes. "As a result, they get no practice in handling conflict. . . . Overprotection prevents them from learning the skills necessary to avoid exploitation by others."[29]

Being perceived as gay. For some reason, calling someone "gay" or a "fag"—whether they are gay or not—has become a common insult. Little children who do not even know what those words mean may hurl them at each other. Teenagers who understand the concept of homosexuality, and who may have been in discussions about tolerance, still often use those words to hurt people. Whether the person is actually gay does not seem to matter.

According to one dance teacher, boys often drop out of dance classes, even though they are interested in dance, because they are teased and bullied about being gay. He had a student who confessed he did not want to go to school anymore because he was so tormented. "He was actually beaten up several times, all because he danced," the teacher wrote. "He said his classmates—boys and girls alike— were always calling him a fag. He was dealing with it day in and day out, and it had obviously had a major emotional effect on him." The teacher said this student's experience reminded him of his own past. He wrote:

> *I had been through the same torment this kid was enduring. I can remember sneaking out the back door of my junior high school to avoid the bullies who would think nothing of giving me a punch or two and calling me a fag every time they had the opportunity.*[30]

When teens actually are gay, the bullying becomes worse. Public attention to this issue in the media has grown in recent years, with the bullying of a gay high school student becoming a major plot thread in the hit television series *Glee*. The 2011 National School Climate Survey by the Gay, Lesbian & Straight Education Network (GLSEN), which tracks social attitudes over time, found that over 80 percent of teens who are gay reported being verbally harassed for their sexual orientation. Nearly 40 percent reported being physically harassed, and nearly 20 percent reported being physically assaulted. Fortunately, there has been progress against this type of bullying in recent years. The GLSEN survey also shows the percentage of students hearing homophobic remarks frequently has declined over the past decade, while 2011 showed a significant decrease in harassment and assault. Students also report an increase in access to support and resources.[31]

Understanding Why Some Victims Fight Back

Randi, the now-adult woman who was ignored and bullied as a child, says she can understand why some victims finally react violently. She says:

Family and friends gather at a vigil at the Columbine Memorial for the ten-year anniversary of the tragedy.

Kids who go in and shoot people—I can very easily understand why they do that. I would never do such a thing, but I can understand how somebody could. When you are in the position of being bullied you do a lot of fantasizing about hurting people in return. In the back of my mind I think, "If you did anything like what I experienced, then you deserve it. It is hard for me to feel sorry for you."[32]

Why should society care if bullying goes on? Randi offers some insights into how a victim feels. But not only victims are affected by bullying; the bullies are also. In the next chapter we will look at both the short-term and the long-term effects of bullying on both bullies and their victims.

4

How Bullying Affects Both Bullies and Victims

I feel as if I'm going to explode. I have never experienced anger like this before. . . . I go to the kitchen, open the drawer. . . . I pull out the largest knife. I hold it up. . . . I'm going to cut out . . . the hearts of everyone [who] hurt me. . . . I want to kill them like they're killing me.[1]

Those are the words of Jodee Blanco, a young woman who was bullied throughout her childhood. The experience was so hard for her that when she was an adult she wrote a book about it called *Please Stop Laughing at Me.*

Blanco's words tell us about one thing that bullying does: It causes immediate anger on the part of the victim. But bullying does more than just make the victim mad:

> *About sixty years ago . . . we lived across the alley from a little girl named Daisy and her family. One day I was walking home from school with a couple of friends and Daisy was walking ahead of us by herself. My friends told me to run up and hit Daisy. I didn't really want to, but peer pressure won out, and I did as they said. Daisy showed more character than I did. She did not respond in any way. I have never forgiven myself for this act of bullying. Children are hurt easily and even though it's been sixty years, the incident has preyed on my conscience, and I'm sure Daisy hasn't forgotten it either. I hope Daisy has had a wonderful life and has forgiven this stringy-haired little kid who can't forget her.[2]*

Those words were written to a newspaper advice column by someone who bullied many years ago. In this case, the bully regrets her actions, and that lifelong regret has remained with her.

Bullying has many effects, both on the bully and the victim. Those effects are both short-term and long-term.

Short-Term Effects on the Victim

What Jodee Blanco expressed was rage at being victimized, rage that came on as the bullying was happening. That is called a short-term effect. It is not the only one. William Voors, a family counselor and consultant to schools on bullying, lists a number of short-term effects of being bullied.[3]

• Low self-confidence: Kids who are bullied think they cannot do anything about it. That can lead to feelings of inferiority, of not being able to do much about problems in general.

• Depression: Victims can become depressed, feeling sad and hopeless. That feeling can worsen into a true clinical depression. Depression is defined as "an abnormal emotional state characterized by exaggerated feelings of sadness, melancholy, dejection, worthlessness, emptiness, and hopelessness that are inappropriate, out of proportion to reality."[4]

• Suicidal thoughts and suicide attempts: A survey by the British organization Kidscape said that 20 percent of victims of bullying reported at least one attempt to kill themselves.[5] Another study that looked at over four hundred teenagers found that depression and thoughts of suicide were more common among bullying victims.[6]

• Abnormal fears and worries: As a victim becomes afraid of a bully, he or she may become crippled by fear in general.

• Sleep disorders: The victim may not be able to sleep due to stress, or may sleep more and more as a way to escape.

• Nervous habits: Eye twitches, nail and lip biting, hair chewing—the list of nervous habits victims can have goes on and on.

• Frequent crying: When children cry, a bully may be provoked to resort to even meaner taunts to make them cry even more.

• Bed-wetting: Anxiety and tension can show up in physical symptoms like bed-wetting. That may make the victim feel even worse about himself or herself.

• Poor appetite or digestive problems: The stomachache that makes a student want to stay home from school may be caused by a bully rather than a virus.

• School problems: Victims may be so worried about bullying they are not able to study. Their grades may fall, and they may stop saying anything in class.

• Rage: Sometimes rage against those doing the bullying can become extreme. In some horrifying incidents, kids have taken guns or other weapons to school as a response to being bullied. The U.S. Secret Service has reviewed many cases of school shootings. They found that two thirds of the attackers had felt persecuted, bullied, threatened, attacked, or injured by others. Many of them had been the victims of severe bullying.[7]

Dr. Bruce Nerenberg says:

> *Victims begin to see themselves in the victim role. . . . They can stay in that role their whole lives, making bad choices that keep them in the victim role. Or they can suddenly become aggressive. The anger and resentment wells up so much that they themselves become aggressive and take it out on somebody else.*[8]

"Phil" (not his real name) is an example of this:

> *I was bullied like crazy as a kid because I had polio. When I had surgery in fourth grade things changed. Within a year I could walk and I became, if not a bully, then a force to be reckoned with. By that time, I was so angry that if I did get into a fight I was downright dangerous. All those years on crutches had built my upper body to fearsome strength. Every night I did three hundred sit-ups in bed just to burn off the rage. Because I could walk but not run, I knew that when I went into a fight that I had better be able to win. As a result, the few fights I had seemed like fights to the death. Both I and my opponent were very lucky that there were always other people around to pull us apart. I believe that every fight I ever had was in response to a bully who still thought of me as a "cripple."*[9]

The short-term effects of being bullied do not make a pretty picture. Neither do the long-term effects.

Long-Term Effects on the Victim

> *I am . . . scared to go [to a high school reunion]. . . . I'm terrified to get out of this car because I know inside . . . are ghosts from my past. . . . They destroyed my self-worth so much that it's taken me twenty years to stop hating myself. . . . They probably don't even remember half of what they did to me. In their minds, they were just kids being kids. . . . They took something vital from [me]. It's taken me my whole adult life to get it back.*[10]

The effects of bullying have been so long lasting that Jodee Blanco was afraid to go to her high school reunion.

Because victims are so afraid of being bullied again, they may form personality traits that keep them isolated from their peers. While no one likes a bully, it seems that victims are not very popular either. Dr. Marano says, "These children [victims] internalize the very negative views of themselves others hold of them."[11]

Dr. Dan Olweus, a social science researcher in Norway who did much of the original research on bullying, found that by the time bullied children become adults, some "normalization" takes place. Victims are freer to choose or create their own social life. At the same time, he said, they are still at risk for depression and negative feelings about themselves.[12]

Another researcher found that adults who had been victims of bullying in childhood reported higher levels of loneliness than did non-victims. In addition, that study showed that adult men who never married and were shy with women often had a history of being bullied in childhood. That suggests the social withdrawal often seen in victims may continue in later life.[13]

Of course, it is not always that way. Many children, perhaps most of them, who are bullied grow up to be normal, happy people. But for some, the fear and self-hatred caused by the bullies never leave.

Short-Term Effects on the Bully

It would seem logical that the effects of bullying are worse for the victim than the bully. After all, the bully is getting his way and is on top in the "pecking order." However, studies show that being a bully is not good for a child any more than being a victim is.

"There are huge costs to [bullies]," writes Dr. Marano. She points out that while bullies often think of themselves as popular because they get their way so much, they do not know or understand what other kids really think of them.[14]

Marano cites Dr. Olweus's research that found that up to grade six, bullies are of average popularity, but after that things change. "As they get older [bullies'] popularity with classmates wanes. . . . They

The effects of bullying on the victim can include anxiety, depression, and even suicidal thoughts.

may get what they want through aggression, and be looked up to for being tough, but they are not *liked*."[15]

Their very toughness, says researcher Dr. Melissa DeRosier, prevents them from understanding why other kids do not like them. "As something of a threat to others, they are not likely to learn just exactly how other kids feel about them," she says. "They certainly don't see the impact of their own behavior on others."[16]

Since schools today are monitoring bullying much more closely, bullies may also find themselves in the principal's office more often. They may be given detentions or other punishments or even suspended from school. Their parents may be notified about their behavior, and that may mean punishment at home.

Long-Term Effects on the Bully

What can a person who bullies others in childhood or adolescence look forward to? For many of them, of course, a perfectly normal life. Some bullies "grow out of" the behavior and become successful adults.

But some do not.

Peter Sheras writes, "Though bullies do frequently enjoy a certain status in the early and middle school years, their popularity starts to decrease sharply in their late teens."[17]

As bullies grow into adults, their bullying personalities can cause even greater problems. "As adults [bullies] frequently find themselves disliked, dissatisfied and even in trouble with the law," Sheras continues.[18]

"The person hurt most by bullying is the bully himself," writes Dr. Marano. "Most bullies have a downwardly spiraling course through life," she continues. "Bullies . . . are far more likely than nonaggressive kids to commit crimes, batter their wives, abuse their children—and produce another generation of bullies."[19]

Many different studies support her conclusion. Negative effects of bullying on the bullies include many troublesome problems.

Trouble with the law. Dr. Olweus found that 60 percent of boys who were named as bullies by their peers in grades six to nine have at least one court conviction by age twenty-four.[20]

A psychologist from the University of Michigan, Leonard Eron, followed 518 children in upstate New York starting at age eight; they are now adults in their forties. The ones who were named by the other students at age eight as the most aggressive committed more crimes (and more serious crimes) as adults than the children who were not bullies. They also were more likely than children not named as bullies to have more driving offenses, court convictions, alcoholism, and antisocial personality disorders, and they were more likely to use mental health services.[21]

Dr. Eron, commenting on the results of his study, said, "Those youngsters at age eight who are aggressive often continue to be so at age nineteen, at age thirty. They do not achieve as much socially. They don't get as much education and don't experience as much success in their careers."[22]

Academic problems. A researcher in Montreal, Canada, has been following a thousand bullies and aggressive kids to see how they fare as they get older. "Aggression leads increasingly to rejection by peers, parents, even the school system," he writes. "By the end of elementary school, half of bullies are not in their age-appropriate grade."[23] Difficulty in school can also be a cause of bullying; the two can work together to make the situation worse.

Mental health issues. Bullies, as well as their victims, can suffer from depression. The study on depression in bullies and victims found that bullies also had higher rates of depression than the normal population. "Depression was equally likely to occur among those who were bullied and those who were bullies," the researchers wrote. "[Thoughts of suicide] occurred most often among the adolescents who were bullies."[24]

Unpopularity and social isolation. The same researchers also found that bullies were more likely to be rejected by their peers and suffer social isolation.[25]

Does it sound like both bullies and victims are doomed to a lifetime of unhappiness? That is not necessarily the case. Bullies can give up their aggressive behaviors and form normal, healthy friendships. And victims can grow stronger as they learn to cope with bullies and value themselves.

Jodee Blanco writes, "The pain I went through as a teen strengthened me and taught me the truth of that wonderful adage about doing unto others as you would wish them to do unto you."[26]

When Girls Bully

Alex was starting the fifth grade at a new school.

It was a small school. There were just sixteen kids in my class. The girls wouldn't accept me. They wouldn't talk to me or anything and every day I was eating lunch all alone. It was the popular group that was doing it. Then they started rumors; they said that I was gay. They called me a lesbian.

Alex was very upset by the way the other girls were treating her, but she decided not to tell anyone about it. "I didn't feel good about it, but I didn't tell," she says. "I don't know why, I just didn't feel comfortable telling anybody. Then I got to be friends with a couple of other girls who didn't get along with the popular group either and I started eating lunch with them."

Alex's mother was a teacher at the same school, but she had no idea what was going on. Alex says:

> One of my friends told my mother. My mother talked to my teacher about it and they did some things to make it stop. I had to give the teacher the names of the girls. They had to talk to her, and then they had to see the guidance counselor. They were mad about it. After that happened it kept going on, but eventually it did stop.

Now in sixth grade, things are somewhat better, she says:

> I do have a group of friends. The popular girls talk to me, but they still aren't exactly the nicest. I think they know how bad it was. From what I know, they aren't doing that particular thing to anyone now, but they still aren't so nice to some other kids. They just think they rule the whole class! We're not good friends now, but I can talk to them. I sit by one of them in band. I get along with her OK, but it's still not that great.[1]

Boys and girls can have very different styles of bullying. Generally, boys are quicker to use physical means: fighting, pushing, hurting someone physically. Generally, girls use a different way of bullying: teasing, excluding someone, not talking to her, spreading rumors.

That does not mean that boys never spread rumors or make another boy feel left out—they do. It does not mean that girls never push, hit, or kick another girl—they do. It just means that boys use physical force more often while girls use less physical methods.

Some researchers have given what girls do a name. They call it "relational aggression." Recently, social scientists have been looking at relational aggression to try to understand what it is, how it works, and what it does to victims.

One researcher, Rachel Simmons, interviewed hundreds of junior high and high school girls and describes girl bullying in her book.

> Girls use backbiting, exclusion, rumors, name-calling, and manipulation to inflict psychological pain on targeted victims. . . . Girls frequently attack within tightly knit networks of friends.

Bullying among teen girls tends to consist of 'relational aggression'—teasing, isolating or excluding someone, or spreading rumors—rather than physical force

. . . Within the hidden culture of aggression, girls fight with body language and relationships. . . . There is no gesture more devastating than the back turning away.[2]

Before we deal with the aggression that girls display toward each other, we need to understand something about the social structure of a typical group or classroom of girls. Many readers will recognize their own class in this description.

Insiders and Outsiders

Ask any middle or high school girl if there are cliques in her school and the answer will almost always be "yes." But what exactly is a clique? To some, it is just a bunch of friends who like to hang out together. To others, it is an exclusive group that rigidly controls who is "in" and who is "out." Common in most schools, cliques most often form in sixth, seventh, and eighth grades.

A researcher who wrote a book about girl bullying, Rosalind Wiseman, watched cliques in various school settings for many years, and from that she has drawn up a list of the roles girls often play in cliques. Girls may interact differently at your school, but generally, she says, girls fall into one of seven roles:

• Queen Bee: This is the most popular girl in the class; she runs everything, and everyone seems to do her bidding.

• Sidekick: The Queen Bee's best friend; she will always back the Queen in everything.

• Banker: She collects information about other girls, especially their secrets, and gives it to others when she or the clique can gain something from it.

• Floater: This girl does not belong exclusively to any one group but has friends in all groups and can move freely between them. She is willing to stand up to the Queen Bee and is often the happiest because she does not have to worry about hanging on to her position in one group.

• Torn Bystander: This is a girl with a conscience. She understands when the clique is doing something nasty and is

43

torn between her loyalty to the clique and doing the right thing. Sometimes she is the go-between when other girls have a conflict.

• Pleaser/Wannabe/Messenger: This girl really wants to be in the clique but usually is not invited in. She will do anything for the Queen Bee and will always stand up for her. She often serves as a messenger—carrying messages from one to the other when two girls are in a fight.

• Target, or Odd Girl Out: This is the girl the others pick on, the one who is humiliated, made fun of, excluded. She is often described as a "loser."[3]

Rachel Simmons does not see the clique in terms of such clear-cut roles, but rather sees it as a group of girls building alliances. The most popular girls, she says, build a group around them and use it to increase their popularity and put down others who challenge them.[4]

Why do girls join such a group? Because, Simmons says, it gives them a chance to belong, even for a short while, to a clique. Being able to turn other girls against a target makes them more popular. Alliance building and cliques, she points out, encourage other types of relational aggression such as rumor spreading and telling secrets.[5]

The result of relational aggression is that school becomes a "minefield" in which girls must constantly keep track of which girl is on which side and negotiate their own places, Simmons writes. "With little or no warning a clique will rise up and cut down one of its own. For the targeted girl, the sheer force of this unexpected expulsion can be startling, unpredictable, and devastating."[6]

What We Know About Relational Aggression

One academic study looked at twenty adolescent girls to try to better understand relational aggression. The girls were interviewed and answered a questionnaire. The researchers found many interesting things about girl bullying.

• The most common forms of relational aggression were being excluded from the peer group and having lies told about them. Name-calling was also common.

A clique can be seen as a bunch of friends with similar interests, or as an exclusive group with rigid roles and rules.

- Most girls described more than one incident of being a victim. The bullying happened most often at school but sometimes on the bus or in the neighborhood.
- Insults about weight, race, or other characteristics were common.
- Being new or different in some way made the chance of being a victim greater.
- Most girls reported feeling sad, hurt, or rejected when they were a victim.
- A few girls of various ages said they had cried. Others said they tried not to cry because that would mean more teasing.
- Some girls said they ignored the bully and what she did, but others said they responded with words or with physical actions like pushing or slapping.
- Many girls said they had to work hard to "hold themselves back" from responding with words or actions.
- Only about a quarter of the girls said they went to a teacher or parent for help.
- Some girls said the bullying lowered their self-esteem, especially those who were teased about being overweight.
- Many girls said they had lost friendships because of bullying.[7]

The "Big P": Popularity

Why are girls sometimes so mean to each other? Mostly it is the quest to be popular—to be the leader and to be looked up to.

Rachel Simmons says:

> [Popularity] is a cutthroat contest into which girls pour boundless energy and anxiety. . . . They lie to be accepted, cheat their friends by using them, steal people's secrets to resell at a higher social price. At its core, popularity is a mean and merciless competition.[8]

Many kids think that the popular girls are those who are the most liked. That is not always true, another group of researchers say. They found the most popular students actually were the best-liked in early elementary school, but things changed in middle school. They reported:

> *We were told that popular people were the most visible in the school; they were the students most people knew by name. In fact, the popular kids may actually be disliked by a fair number of their classmates. That's because the popular kids feel their popularity will be diminished if they are seen with unpopular kids. To the popular kid, popularity is like a white T-shirt while everyone around them has purple paint on their hands. If they associate with those less desirable students, their paint will sully that white popularity T-shirt and ruin it.*[9]

In order to maintain their status, popular girls need to be seen only with "cool" kids. That makes them snub less popular people. That can build a lot of resentment around them.[10]

What makes a girl popular? It is a combination of many factors. Most of the reasons are quite shallow. Looks are certainly highest on the list—most popular girls are pretty. Being thin and having the right clothes and hairstyle are all important. Years ago, popular girls did not play sports, but that has changed. Athletic ability now counts; being a cheerleader counts even more. Here are some comments from kids about what makes people popular.

"You have to talk a lot. If you don't talk a lot nobody knows who you are."

"You have to hang out with the right people."

"How you dress is important. The 'little people'—the ones who don't talk, the odd ones—they always dress different."[11]

In December 2000, a survey sponsored by Liz Claiborne, the fashion designer, and the Empowerment Program, a school program to raise girls' self-esteem, asked 477 fourteen to seventeen-year-olds about popularity and cliques at their schools. Again, they got interesting information.

- Seventy-seven percent of the teens thought that some groups of students in their schools were "above the rules."

Among teenagers, physical attractiveness plays an important part in popularity.

- Eighty-six percent thought that certain students had more influence with their classmates than others did.
- Thirty-six percent said that students with the most influence (the popular group) often intimidate and embarrass students who are not part of the group.
- Only one third of the students said that popular people who do mean things to others get into trouble with teachers or school administrators.
- Only 16 percent said that other students try to stop an incident of bullying by popular kids.
- Half said that people who are picked on by the popular group tend to isolate themselves from other students.
- Forty percent said that the student being picked on will usually laugh along with the bully even if he or she is really angry.
- Thirty percent said that victims usually plan ways to get back at their tormentors in the future.[12]

Does it sound like a threatening world, this world of girl bullies? It is. A college professor of psychology said, "Girls very much value intimacy, which makes them excellent friends and terrible enemies. They share so much information when they are friends that they never run out of ammunition if they turn on one another."[13]

What Relational Bullies Actually Do

We have briefly mentioned the backbiting, exclusion, and rumor spreading that girls use to bully those out of favor with the popular clique. Those methods need to be looked at in some depth.

Looks. How people look is really the least important quality on how they should be judged, but in the world of popularity, it is the most important. Many girls are obsessed with their looks, Rosalind Wiseman says. They need constant assurance from each other that they fit in and have the right look. They compare themselves to each other and to role models in the entertainment and fashion world. They know the stars and models they see are not realistic images, but they try to reach that standard anyway. Wiseman writes, "Adolescence is a beauty pageant; everyone is in the pageant regardless of whether they want to be or not."[14]

Differences. People who are different in any way invite being the victim. Girls are under tremendous pressure to fit into the ideal set up by the other girls. MTV, teen magazines, and movie and music stars may set the standards, but those standards are enforced by the girls themselves. Wiseman says that girls "police each other," constantly keeping track of who is breaking the rules on how to look and act.[15] Being of a minority race or religion, having a disability, wearing glasses, or being overweight are all differences that cause girls to be victims.

The "gay" issue. For some reason, calling girls gay or labeling them lesbians is an often-used insult. It really has nothing to do with whether or not the girl actually is gay. Sometimes younger kids hurling the insult do not even understand the meaning of the word lesbian—a woman who is sexually attracted to other women. A girl who is very athletic or who does not fit the "in" feminine look may be labeled gay. Wiseman says girls have told her about being tripped, shoved, and pushed down stairs while being called gay.[16] Some schools are now requiring students who use this form of insult to go to classes about understanding and accepting differences.

Conceit. Calling a girl conceited, full of herself, or, in the slang phrase, saying that she "thinks she's all that" is a powerful weapon. To avoid being labeled, girls often run themselves down while complimenting others. "I'm so fat, but you look so good," a girl may say to a friend. The girl saying it may not really think she is fat (or that her hair is awful or whatever else she is using) but saying so is a way to prove she is not conceited.

Exclusion/isolation/not being invited. The target girl is the one who sits alone at lunch, walks home alone, or sits by herself on the bus. She is never invited to the really cool parties. Some target girls find friends among the unpopular group; that can help. But the group may be built largely on dislike for the popular kids.

Adults are not always aware of what is going on socially among teens, which can make it difficult for them to put a stop to relational bullying.

It is not just the unpopular girls who can be isolated. The popular girl who crosses someone above herself in the pecking order may find herself suddenly isolated, friendless, and alone. For someone who used to be in the popular group to suddenly find herself outside looking in can be a devastating experience. It may affect her self-esteem and leave her depressed. Some girls to whom this happens carry the hurt and anger well into adulthood.

Rumors, telling secrets. The girl who confides to a friend that she likes a certain guy may not want it to be all over school the next day—but it might be. Woe to the girl who tells a friend that she does not like another girl—by lunchtime the whole class may have taken sides in the "big fight." Rumors about a girl's sexual experience may lead to her getting the worst label of all.

"Slut"—the nuclear label. Wiseman says the reputation of being a slut can upset even those girls at the top of the social hierarchy.[17] Wearing suggestive clothes and too much makeup and being too interested in boys can all lead to the label. Since today's fashions are often suggestive and most girls wear makeup and like boys, a girl is walking a tightrope. Where the line between attractive, sexy, and slutty lies can be a real mystery. Schools have discovered how hard the line is to define when they have tried to put dress codes in place. One store for young teens created a great deal of controversy when it marketed sexy underwear to girls as young as age ten.

One writer, Emily White, interviewed hundreds of girls who had been labeled as sluts in school to learn more about what happens to a girl who is stuck with that reputation, deserved or not. While she wrote a whole book on the subject, here is a summary of what she found:

> When a girl has been labeled the slut, other kids don't want to get near her. . . . Both girls and boys . . . keep themselves apart from the slut, create a safe distance. Even if boys claim to have slept with her . . . to show any loyalty to her would be to make themselves contaminated too. Girls who at one time might have been friends

with the slut recede . . . they need to be careful how they associate with her or they will be thought of as sluts along with her.[18]

How Teachers Deal With Girls Who Bully

Relational bullying can be especially hard for a teacher or a school to deal with because it is so "under the radar screen." Many times teachers simply do not know what is going on—in Alex's case, her mother was a teacher at the same school and did not see it.

In one school, the problem became so severe the principal had to call in outside help. "It started with girls in the fifth grade picking on one girl—name-calling, she couldn't wear anything right, say anything right, or even bring anything for lunch right," says Mary Irish, principal of a small, private school. "She tried at first to just ignore it, but it started to spread like the tentacles of an octopus. Some kids felt sorry for the one who was being picked on and pretty soon three or four others found themselves also the brunt of jokes, comments, and unkind things."

The principal is not even sure why the original girl was targeted. "She didn't have the earmarks of what I call the typical 'bunny'— bunnies are passive, they'll run away and hide but they won't retaliate. She wasn't shy, she wasn't unattractive," she recalls. "I think they just saw her as an easy mark and they may have known that her mother would react pretty violently." She did indeed, calling the other girls' parents and complaining.

Finally, when the teachers complained that the situation was getting in the way of education, Irish called in a psychologist to try to correct the problem. The psychologist met with the faculty, talked to the girls themselves, and set up a meeting with the parents. "She told the parents that this was a very serious problem," Irish says. "She asked every parent to go home and lay it on the line with their kids: This is what the victims are feeling and this has got to stop."

For the rest of the semester, the faculty watched the girls closely—"We wore those kids like a second skin," Irish says. "No one was ever unattended in the hall, in the classroom, wherever they were." By the next year, in sixth grade, things were better. There were two sections of sixth grade; the school divided the students so the ringleaders were separated, although they were still together for PE and lunch. "I'm not going to say we never had incidents, but maybe some maturity had kicked in and it was better," she says.

Her advice to victims? "You can't just take it; the sooner you tell, the sooner we can stem the flood," she says.[19] We will look at ways to do that in a later chapter.

What can girls do themselves to stop this kind of behavior? One option is to confront the mean girl who is the leader. Here are some suggestions on how to do that. For more information, see chapter 7 on dealing with a bully.

- Write down the details of the teasing or meanness including the date and what was said so when you face the bully, you will have examples of what she has been doing.
- Practice in front of a mirror. Keep your tone of voice calm, eyes steady, and body language confident but not confronting.
- Pick a place and time where you can talk to the person alone, but where you feel safe (like the school library). You do not want to do it in front of her friends because that will cause her to lose face and make her behavior worse.
- Describe exactly what is bothering you.
- Tell the person what you want her to do and not to do.
- Tell the person you like her and would like to be friends, if that is true. It is always good to end with a compliment.[20]

Another way might be to join an activity in which popular girls and targets work together. "I've seen girls who had labeled each other as dorks, nerds, sluts, or heads come to be best friends by participating in sports, band, or clubs together," says one teacher. "I've seen girls in my classes find out that the labels they had tagged each other with were totally wrong."[21]

When dealing with relational bullying, it is always good to remember that the situation will not go on forever. Everyone in time moves on to a new school, with a chance to start over. "All of the senior girls I talked to said that one of the main things they are looking forward to when they go off to college in September is being able to start anew and shed all of the labels they acquired from other girls," says the same teacher.[22]

Anti-Bullying Programs at School

Logan, age eight, saw a play about bullying at his school. Asked what he had learned from it, he said, "I wouldn't stand by and watch someone be bullied because that's mean."[1]

Maybe Logan would have thought that before he saw the play. But maybe he would not have. The play he watched was just one example of the things schools are doing to try to stop bullying.

Bullies, of course, have always existed. And school has always been their number one place to operate. While most schools were aware of bullying, the issue did not seem to be a priority until a series of school shootings focused attention on the problem. Some parents have filed lawsuits against schools when their child was injured by a bully. That has also made schools more aware of the need to confront bullying problems.

Research on how schools could prevent bullying started in the early 1990s. Much of it was done in Norway by Dr. Dan Olweus, a university professor there. The school system in Norway is similar to that of the United States, so U.S. schools have been able to use his research and the prevention program he wrote. Today there are many different programs put out by different companies for schools to choose from.

But before any school can put a bullying-prevention program in place, the staff needs to know that bullying is a problem in their school. Unless the students tell them, they will not know. And students' record of telling teachers or principals when they or someone they know is being bullied is not very good. According to the Liz Claiborne study mentioned in chapter 5, less than one third—31 percent—of students in the survey said that victims usually report bullying to someone at school.[2]

Another study done in several Midwestern schools showed that while teachers could accurately identify 50 percent of the bullies in their school, they were able to pick out only 10 percent of the victims.[3]

Why is that? Probably because the students are embarrassed and ashamed to be the victims of bullies. They may be afraid that if they tell someone they will be called a "tattletale" or a "snitch" and may be picked on even more. Children who see someone being bullied may be afraid to tell anyone for the same reasons.

Teachers and school principals may look the other way because they do not want to confront the problem. "Teachers and principals underestimate the amount of bullying in schools and, when they do witness it, often are reluctant to get involved," says Nan Stein, one researcher. "Kids say that when they tell the adults about the bullying, adults don't take them seriously, or they make them feel responsible for going back and working it out."[4]

In the Norwegian research, 40 percent of elementary students and 60 percent of junior high school students said that teachers tried to stop bullying only "once in a while" or "almost never."[5]

Almost all state legislatures have stepped in and authorized school districts to put bullying-prevention programs in place. In 1999, Georgia was the first state to do so. The legislature in Colorado, home of Columbine High School, ordered every district in the state to have a program in place by the end of 2001. As of 2012, Montana is the only state with no anti-bullying law.[6]

We will look at a typical bullying-prevention program and discuss how similar programs are working in two schools.

How a Typical Program Is Set Up

Just telling bullies to stop or telling victims to ignore them or fight back are not solutions to a school's bullying problem, experts say. "To prevent bullying, educators need to do nothing less than change the school culture," says researcher J. David Hawkins, "the social environment in which learning takes place."[7]

According to Dr. Olweus, that has to be done in three levels in a school: the whole-school level, the classroom level, and the individual level.[8]

The whole-school level. A school needs to start by making the entire school, students and staff, aware of the anti-bullying effort. The first step usually is to have students fill out a survey without putting their names on it. Students can use it to safely tell the school administration about bullying in their school. It may ask questions like these:

- Have you ever been bullied at our school?
- What kind of bullying happens here?
- Does bullying happen often here?
- How many times in the last month have you been bullied?
- Do the teachers know about the bullying?
- Do they do anything to stop it?

Once the teachers and principal have the results of the survey, they usually have an all-school meeting in which they tell students about the results. Students are sometimes shocked to find out how much bullying is going on in their school. Sometimes students also watch a video or see a play about bullying.

The next step is to put some all-school policies in place. They may include telling students that teachers who see bullying will no longer ignore it, but will step in to stop it. Supervision by teachers and aides in the halls, lunchroom, and playground may be increased because research shows that the more teachers and aides per pupil, the lower the rate of bullying.[9] Some larger schools have set up a phone number students can call to report bullying. Others may use a box where students can put notes about being bullied. Sometimes, if the bullying problem is very bad, parents may be asked to come to a meeting to talk about it.

In addition, many schools prepare a plan to deal with a bully that lays out steps that will be taken for each offense. Those can vary from school to school; later in this chapter we will look at such plans at two middle schools.

The classroom level. Teachers can try to create a better "climate" in their individual classrooms in several ways. They can have students sit down together and talk about bullying. Younger children may need to have the terms "bully" and "victim" explained to them. Older children will probably know quite well what they mean. Children may brainstorm ideas for rules about bullying in their room, and from those ideas they can draw up a list of "Rules for Our Classroom." The rules do not have to be complicated, especially for younger children. They may be as simple as:

- In our classroom we will not bully other students.
- We will all try to help other students who are being bullied.
- We will try to include students who are left out.[10]

Teachers may read their students books or stories about bullies and victims. They may have the children role-play situations. If children have a chance to act out both the bully and the victim, it

Teachers and other staff members are working to prevent bullying in school. Part of the problem has been that many teachers cannot tell when bullying is going on.

can help them understand why bullying hurts. They may do a lot of group discussion, encouraging children to express how it feels to be a bully or to be a victim. The same things may be done with older students on a more advanced level. Teachers may go out of their way to praise students when they see someone being nice to a child who is left out.

Teachers also may have students talk about seeing bullying happening and not doing anything to stop it. They can explore the reasons why bystanders may not be willing to help or to report the bullying. The teacher may explain to the students that telling someone in authority when bullying happens is not "tattling" but is done to take the side of the victim and prevent someone from being hurt.[11]

The individual level. Since the purpose of the program is to stop bullying, students who bully need to be dealt with quickly and firmly. The school staff must make it clear that bullying will not be tolerated. A system of consequences may be set up. Often the consequences are in steps, laying out what will be done for a first, second, and third offense. The actual consequences vary from school to school depending on how severe the problem is. They often include a conference with the principal or guidance counselor, detention, notifying the parents, suspension, or, in severe cases, even calling the police. All of these consequences risk making a bully even more angry and alienated from school. However, without consequences it is difficult to change behavior.

Some schools have started programs for victims too, trying to give them better social skills and help them learn to make friends.

Looking at Two School Programs

Michael Bralick, principal of Butler Middle School in Wisconsin, says, "I don't think we were any worse than other schools [about bullying], but the more you read about what bullying causes, the more it seemed that something had to be done."[12]

Rather than use a purchased anti-bullying program, Bralick decided to create a program just for his school. The teachers worked with him. He describes his school's anti-bullying effort as a "respect" program.

They decided to begin at a very simple level with developing friendship skills. "Nobody is teaching kids how to make friends anymore," says Marianne Kirsh, the school's special education teacher. "We just assume that when you are in elementary school you learn that. Well, some kids don't."[13] All the teachers in the school spent time with their classes, discussing how to be a friend and things to do and not do in order to make and keep friends.

The school began a diversity group in which students discuss differences in people such as race, religion, disability, and culture. The group did awareness activities at the whole-school level such as a wall mural, posters, announcements on the public address system, and skits.

Then the school moved to the specific issue of bullying. All students met in an assembly for a presentation on bullying and its effects. "We told the kids that nobody has the right to make you feel miserable here in our school because if you don't want to come to school, you aren't going to learn," Bralick says. "We looked at kids with high absentee rates—are they victims and they're not letting us know? We told kids, if we don't know about it, we can't cure it. We tried to get all the kids in the building to have more empathy."[14]

Students took a bullying survey. Teachers did activities on bullying in class. They encouraged their students to discuss the effects of bullying and helped students to understand how being bullied feels. They talked about telling an adult rather than standing by when they see bullying happen.

One of the school's regularly scheduled parent meetings dealt with the topic of bullying.

When teachers saw a student bullying another student, they stepped in and stopped it. Repeat offenders met with the principal; sometimes parents were called in.

Beginning in the early elementary grades, students can learn to work together cooperatively to resist bullying.

"I think the kids are aware now that bullying is not a rite of passage," says Bralick.[15]

A different middle school a few miles away, Wisconsin Hills, set up a more formal anti-bullying program with the steps in dealing with a bully carefully laid out.

"Our seventh grade class had a large number of students who were harassing other students," says Debbie Stears, the guidance counselor. "What we were doing was not effective because the problem was continuing. We realized it had to be part of a whole-school plan."[16]

"A lot of it was going on under the radar. The kids weren't getting any consequences because what they were doing didn't come up to the level for discipline," adds Pat Haislmaier, the school psychologist. "We really needed to address the below-the-radar type of bullying that we weren't addressing at all."[17]

"We also had a high incidence of kids not reporting bullying because it was tattling," explains Ceil Carse, a special education teacher at the school. "We had to let them know that it's OK to tell someone when you are being bullied. It's not OK to be a victim of bullying."[18]

Their program is similar in the beginning to other schools' programs. They do many of the same activities: such as giving a survey, having an assembly to explain the anti-bullying policy, and working in the classrooms to teach students about the issue. Where they are different is in the set of formal consequences they have put in place.

When a student is caught bullying the first time, he or she is warned that such behavior will not be tolerated. If it happens again, the student meets individually or in a group (depending on how many students are involved) with the social worker or some other staff person. "We start by saying, 'I know what's happened but tell me about it in your own words,'" says Susan McDonald, the school social worker. She says:

> *We start by discussing the situation and reviewing all the key terms like teasing, empathy, physical aggression, verbal aggression, and bullying. We start to connect those to their behavior. Sometimes lights go on—sometimes kids think mean teasing is just kidding. But if the other person isn't laughing, it isn't kidding.[19]*

Then the teacher or social worker introduces what the school calls a "Turn-Around Plan." That is a type of contract that lays out what happened and promises that it will not happen again. The student signs it, the teacher or social worker signs it, and a copy is sent to the parents. The teacher or social worker follows up in two weeks to see if the situation is any better.

If there is a third offense, the school brings in the parents. They are involved in discussing the problem, and they sign a contract with the school to try to stop the behavior.

If the objectionable behavior does not stop, the next step may be suspension from school or even calling the police. This depends on how severe the bullying is. "The parents know that the next step will be suspension or the police," McDonald says. She points out that calling the police does not necessarily mean it will become a legal matter. "We may just have the police liaison person come over and talk to the child and parent about the seriousness of the situation."[20]

"This program started as a kind of reaction to a problem, but we soon discovered that we have to be proactive and also do a prevention piece," says Gina Nau, special education teacher. That part is just as important, if not more so, than dealing with incidents of bullying, she says, describing awareness activities similar to those at Butler Middle School.[21]

Prevention is certainly what school anti-bullying programs intend to accomplish. These programs are much more than just a way to catch and punish bullies. The added intent is to change the whole climate at a school, so that bullying is considered "not cool" anymore.

Remember that old childhood chant, "Sticks and stones can break my bones but names can never hurt me"? Michael Bralick sees it a little differently. "Sticks and stones can break bones," he says, "but names also can break a kid."[22]

Of course, the big question is: Do these programs work? Most schools will give you a "yes, we feel things are better since the program started" answer. Dr. Olweus also researched results. He found a 50 percent reduction in bullying problems during the two years after his anti-bullying program was put in place. The results applied to both boys and girls and to students in all the grades studied—four through nine. There did not seem to be an increase in bullying outside the school. There was also a reduction in antisocial behavior such as fighting and vandalism. Teachers felt there was an improvement in order and discipline in the classrooms and better social relationships between students. Students also said they felt more satisfaction with school life.[23]

Resolving Conflicts Before They Turn to Bullying

Some schools are putting conflict resolution or peer mediation groups in place. The difference between the two is that a conflict resolution plan usually involves a teacher. In a peer mediation program, students are taught to be the leaders to resolve a conflict.

In both cases, students first take time to cool down. Then they describe the conflict to the mediator in their own words. Each side is listened to without commenting on who is right and who is wrong.

Students try to find the reason for the conflict and describe their feelings about it. They brainstorm solutions to the conflict and choose one to try. The mediator checks back in a few days to see how things are going. If the solution is not working, they will try another. They will keep going until they find a solution that makes both people (or groups) happy. Mediators call that a "win-win" solution.[24]

Dealing With a Bully

Gary was in the fifth grade when a bully from the sixth grade began picking on him and his friends. Gary says:

> He would start fights all the time during recess. One time after school he started picking on me and a friend. He was bigger than both of us, but working together we got him down. We were right next to my friend's house, so we got a rope and tied him to a tree with his hands behind him. We hit him in the stomach a couple of times and told him we were sick of him picking on everybody. We left him there, tied to the tree. From that time on, he was a different guy. He didn't pick on us again, he didn't cause fights. Not with us, not with anybody. He knew we weren't afraid of him anymore and that we'd get him one way or the other.[1]

That is one way victims handle a bully. It has more negatives than positives, but it is a way some kids have used.

There are many different ways to cope with bullying; we will explore several of them.

Fighting Back Physically

There are many forms of fighting back: pushing, tripping, hitting. The big question is, does it work? Obviously, in Gary's case it did. However, in many other cases it probably will not.

"Fighting back is the *worst defense*," writes bullying researcher Dr. Marano. "In most instances, victimized children really are weaker and smaller than the bully—thus their fears of losing these fights may be quite real."[2] Some experts would agree with her, but some would not.

Marilyn LaCourt, a family therapist who has worked in bullying prevention, says kids should use a principle called "reciprocity." That means giving back what you have gotten but no more. "When somebody is nice, be nice back," she says. "When somebody is nasty, be nasty back. But don't be more nasty than the other person was nasty to you. If someone takes your hat on the bus, don't let him get away with it. Grab it back or grab his hat, but don't kick him in the shins."[3] Again, some anti-bullying experts would agree with her; others would not.

In a few cases, fighting back has been taken to the most extreme level. In Moses Lake, Washington, a junior high student named Barry Loukaitis walked into algebra carrying a high-powered rifle under his coat. He shot three students and the teacher. The first student he killed had often bullied him. Eric Harris and Dylan Klebold from Columbine High School are another example. They aimed for jocks and other kids who had bullied them.

"As we look at the profile of [school shooters], the majority were first victims. When spurned, rejected, or bullied, some adolescents resort to violence," says Ronald Stephens, the executive director of the National School Safety Center. "They want to resolve their problems quickly and with a measure of finality that is oftentimes rather scary."[4]

Victims who go that far in fighting back pay a terrible price themselves. Some die; those who survive face long jail sentences. Of course, they have caused others terrible suffering. All the experts agree: "Getting even" with a bully is not worth that much pain.

Ignoring, Walking Away

Ever since bullies began picking on kids, mothers have said, "If you just ignore him, he will get tired of it and leave you alone." Most kids' response has probably been, "Oh, Mom, you just don't understand!" However, Mom may have been right.

An Internet source for helping kids cope with bullying offers these suggestions:

- Ignore them: "It may be hard to do at first, but it works," the site says. "Remember these people…want your scared reaction and silence might throw them off. You would have to keep it up for quite a while, but they will get bored and leave you alone."

- Yell and walk away: "You can tell them to buzz off, shout NO or GO AWAY! But you must say it angrily and then walk away immediately. Practice in the mirror."[5]

Another expert, writing an advice column for teens, says:

> *Walk away and ignore the bully. It may seem like a coward's response, but it's not. Bullies thrive on the reaction they get and if you walk away, the message is that you just don't care. Sooner or later the bully will probably get bored with trying to bother you.*[6]

Using Humor

David was bullied in grade school because he was small and not very athletic. Because of a learning disability, he was allowed extra time to take tests, and that made some of his classmates resent him. He found one of the best ways to deal with their bullying was to use his sense of humor. "I've always used humor as part of who I am,"

Many experts agree that fighting back can be a poor way to handle a bully. Oftentimes, it's best to just walk away.

he says. "I still remember the first time I responded to someone bullying me. I said something funny back to him and the other kids laughed. It was like they were saying, 'Touché. Good job.' People laughing made me feel good."[7]

Another grade-schooler was constantly teased about his weight. The other kids called him "Bacon." He tried ignoring them and walking away, but in his case it did not work. Then, one day, when someone shouted "Bacon" at him he turned and said, "Yeah, and I sizzle. I really sizzle." The bully laughed, and the other kids heard him. Things changed that day; the other kids never called him "Bacon" again, and slowly he began to make friends as the others realized he could be fun to be around.[8]

Being Confident

Walking tall and holding your head high so you do not look like a victim waiting to be bullied can help. If you do not feel confident, sign up to take a self-defense course. "[That] will give you more confidence," says the Internet advice site. "These lessons don't necessarily mean you fight back, but they can help your self-confidence."[9]

That is exactly what Marcus did. He says:

> I faced many different kinds of bullying: verbal, physical, you name it. They picked on me because one, I was smarter than them; two, they thought I was pretty ugly; three, they thought I was gay; four, I got better grades than them; and five, I was the new kid. Mostly it was verbal stuff, calling me gay and queer and some swear words that should not be included in the human language. I remember one time when it got physical, though. I was walking out of the double doors to recess and there they were, hanging around the entrance, three or four of them, all bigger than me. One of them came over and pushed me. His friends started closing in around me, but I ran out to the playground away from them.

One of the things Marcus did was to take a self-defense course. "I am currently in Tae Kwon Do and it really boosted my assertiveness and confidence," he says. "I strongly urge kids to get into a self-defense course. It keeps you physically fit and you will not have bullies on your list of worries."[10]

Talking About It

In the Liz Claiborne survey, only about one third of victims reported the bullying to the school and less than one seventh told their parents what was happening to them.[11]

The Secret/*Seventeen* survey found that 22 percent of girls and 13 percent of boys would tell a friend they were being bullied. Only 5 percent of girls and 19 percent of boys would seek support from an adult.[12]

After Marcus ran, the bullies followed and trapped him at the top of the jungle gym. He continues his story:

> *I found an opening in their enclosure and I bolted for the door. I made it to the headmaster's office and I reported them to him. They got two detentions each. My advice to other kids would be, if you are constantly tormented, tell a teacher or an adult. If you see them coming for you, yell for someone to help. I know that may sound like another one of those psychiatrist people, but it is true! All the stuff they tell you to do (like telling) that most kids think is baloney, actually works.*[13]

Jessie was bullied for years in grade school. She went to the same school, with the same group of girls, from first to eighth grade. She says:

> *Right from the get-go there were groups—certain people would hang out with each other. One day they'd hang out with me, the next day they hated me. They would say, "Get away, you freak." That went on until sixth grade. Then, and I don't know why, I really became the outlaw to just about everybody. I wasn't in their image. I didn't wear the right clothes and that stuff. I got nicknames—they called me "Cow." It was really bad. I'd come home from school crying because it really hurt. I was one of the taller girls so I was on the basketball team. During the season I*

was accepted and not made fun of. But after that, it went back to what it used to be.

In eighth grade, she says, it finally got a little better:

I started hanging out with more people, I was accepted a little more. I think by eighth grade you are a little more mature, you see that there is more to a person than outward appearance. I think some of the people who made fun of me, once they got to know me, realized I was not the geek they thought I was.

Her one regret: that she did not tell anyone what was happening. "I didn't tell anyone because I thought that would have made it worse," she says. "I thought if a teacher confronted the people who were doing it, that would make it worse because they would know it was me who told." She did tell her parents, but, she says, they did not know what to do to help her.

In Jessie's opinion:

You need to talk to someone early. Don't hold off. I think that's what hurt me most, that I didn't say anything. If I had said something, it might have stopped. You need to go to the principal or a teacher you trust. I remember another girl in my eighth-grade class who was being made fun of. She talked to her homeroom teacher and he talked to the whole class. He didn't single anybody out, he just said, "We shouldn't be doing this." It got better for her.[14]

Finding Friends

The hardest thing, whether in elementary, middle, or high school, is to be alone. Even having one friend can take the sting out of being bullied. A friend stands up for a victim. A friend offers a listening ear when things are bad.

David says:

Make your own support system. It needs to start at home. Have a good open line of communication with your parents. Then really try to reach out and build relationships with kids your age. Find

One of the hardest things about being a victim is feeling alone. Having a support system of friends to stand beside you can take the sting out of being bullied.

an activity you are good at. All it really takes is a few people to recognize that you do something well. Then you have to take that and just really build on it.[15]

Changing Schools (If All Else Fails)

That may seem like a drastic step, and in many cases it is. But changing schools can be a good thing. It can give a victim a fresh start, a clean slate. David moved to another school district when he was in sixth grade. "It was a very different culture [at the new school] and I felt like I could start fresh," he says:

> *I made an effort. I joined the soccer team and I met some people doing that even though I wasn't the star player. I also joined the Boy Scouts and I had a neighbor in my grade and we became friends. Because I had more friends than at the other school, I felt more comfortable.*[16]

Victims who are still in grade or middle school need to remember that all of life is not grade school. Things often change in high school or college. "Now that I'm in high school, it's gotten a lot better," says Jessie. "I really like it. There are so many people, I hang out with so many different kids. The people that used to make fun of me, I just don't see anymore. You can just be yourself in high school; it's a lot better."[17]

A Word to Bystanders

Kids who stand by and watch when someone else is being bullied are not just observers. They are part of the problem.

One school survey showed that the thing kids worry about most in grades two through six is that they will be harmed or attacked by others.[18] Psychologist Peter Sheras, commenting on that survey, writes, "Students' refusal to tolerate bullying helps decrease this concern, allowing for a more positive attitude toward school, improved social relationships, and better behavior overall."[19]

Though many teens say they would not talk with an adult about problems with a bully, parents and teachers can often help.

Of course, no one is saying that bystanders should physically try to break up a fight. That would be dangerous. The best thing to do in case of a real fight is to tell an adult right away. Then the adult can handle the conflict.

If the bullying is verbal or is done by excluding someone, bystanders need to stand up for the victim. That is very hard to do. Most kids are afraid that if they stand up for the victim, the bullies will turn on them. That can be a very real concern.

However, doing something to stop the bullying or exclusion can bring a reward in several ways.

- It can build courage and self-esteem. It takes a lot of courage to stand up for what is right. Defending someone being bullied or going for help in case of a fight can feel good. Knowing you have done the right thing is very satisfying.

- It can help someone else. Many times bullying starts with just a minor insult. Then it builds, getting worse with every passing day. By stepping in to stop verbal abuse or sitting with someone who is being excluded, you may prevent much greater harm being done to the person later.

- It can avoid guilt. Sometimes bystanders who do nothing feel very guilty later when they find out how badly hurt the victim was. That guilt can haunt someone for years. It is much better to take action and feel a sense of pride.[20]

Taking Legal Action

Some parents have taken the step of calling the police, getting a restraining order (a court order forbidding the bully to come near the victim), or filing a lawsuit when their child is the victim of extreme bullying. There are some questions to ask before taking these steps.

- Is what the bully did a crime? If an adult did the same thing to another adult, would it be considered a crime?
- Is there a real threat to the victim's future safety?
- Is the bullying a one-time thing, or does it go on and on?

- Has the victim tried all the other approaches described above first?

"Police intervention serves as a one-time solution to bullying—an emergency measure to solve a specific, serious problem," writes Dr. Sheras. "It does not generally address the underlying causes of . . . victimization."[21]

Getting a restraining order or filing a lawsuit, he says, can help in rare cases:

> Holding the school system accountable in this way will not undo the harm that has already been done . . . but it can provide [the victim] with the satisfaction of knowing that some form of justice has been done. It can also go a long way toward focusing more attention on the bullying problem at the [victim's] school and other schools.[22]

A Few Words to the Bullies

Bullies need to think carefully about many things. First, they need to know that unchecked bullying may buy them a sense of power for a short time, but will, in the end, do them great damage. Remember the statistics in chapter 4 about the large number of bullies who, in later life, have serious problems with the law? Who do jail time? Or the opinion of the researcher that bullies often do not know it, but they are not liked by other kids?

If you are a bully, you need to deal with several issues.

- What triggers your anger? Bullies need to know what "sets them off." Recognizing what triggers you is the first step to controlling it.

- How does the victim feel? Most bullies seem to have little empathy, or understanding of what others are feeling. If you are a bully, you need to think seriously, and perhaps talk to a victim or counselor, about what effect you have on the victims.

- What other things can you do when angry? Bullies need to have a list of things they can do, other than pick on someone, when angry. Taking a deep breath, yelling in private, punching a punching bag, running or taking part in other exercise, making a joke, talking to a friend, writing a story, drawing a picture, talking to parents or a teacher—every bully's list will be different.[23]

- If you are a girl involved in relational bullying, you especially need to recognize the hurt you are causing in other girls' lives. If you do this because you want to be part of the popular clique, you need to think about what would happen if the group turned on you. Do you really want to be best friends with girls who treat others so meanly?

Society is just beginning to understand the effects of bullying and to learn what to do about it. Every child in elementary, middle, or high school needs to ask, "Am I part of the problem or part of the solution?" When more of us are part of the solution rather than part of the problem, the issue of bullying will no longer devastate as many lives and cause so much pain.

8

Cyberbullying

I've decided to tell you about my never ending story

The words are written by hand on pieces of paper held in the hands of a teenage girl. Her face is mostly cut off by the top of the video screen, showing only her long, dark hair spilling over her bare shoulders as she shows the papers from her stack one by one. Over a gentle acoustic guitar rock song with the words, "May angels lead you in..." the simple black and white image of her hands reveals the details of her experience with cyberbullying. Her original spelling has been maintained:

In 7th grade I would go with friends on webcam
Meet and talk to new people.
Then got called stunning, beautiful, perfect, etc.
Then wanted me to flash ...
So I did ... 1 year later...
I got a msg on facebook
From him ... Don't know how he knew me
It said ... If you don't put on a show for me I will send ur boobs
He knew my adress, school, relatives, friends family names.
Christmas break ...
Knock at my door at 4am ...
It was the police ... my photo was sent to everyone
I then got really sick and got ...
Anxiety, major deppresion and panic disorder
I then moved and got into Drugs & Alcohol ...
My anxiety got worse ... couldn't go out
A year past and the guy came back with my new
list of friends and school. But made a facebook page
My boobs were his profile pic ...
Cried every night, lost all my friends and respect
people had for me ... again...
Then nobody liked me
name calling, Judged ...
I can never get that Photo back
It's out there forever ...
I started cutting ...
I promised myself never again ...
Don't have any friends and I sat at lunch alone
So I moved Schools again.
Everything was better even though I sat still alone
at lunch in the library everday.
After a month later I started talking to an old guy friend
We back and fourth texted and he started to say he ...
Liked me ... Led me on ... He had a girlfriend ...

then he said come over my gf's on vacation
So I did ... huge mistake ...
He hooked up with me ...
I thought he liked me ...
1 week later I get a text get out of your school ...
His girlfriend and 15 others came including hiself
The girl and 2 others just said look around nobody likes you
In front of my new school (50) people ...
A guy than yelled just punch her already
So she did ... she threw me to the ground a punched me several
    times
Kids filmed it. I was all alone and left on the ground.
I felt like a joke in this world ... I thought nobody deserves this :/
I was alone ... I lied and said it was my fault and my idea
I didn't want him getting hurt, I thought he really liked me
but he just wanted the sex ... Someone yelled punch her already
Teachers ran over but I just went and layed in a ditch and my dad
    found me.
I wanted to die so bad ... when he brought me home I drank
    bleach ...
It killed me inside and I thought I was gonna actully die.
Ambulence came and brought me to the hospital and flushed
    me
After I got home all I saw was on facebook - she deserved it, did
    you wash the mud out of your hair? - I hope shes dead
Nobody cared ... I moved away to another city to my moms.
another school ... I didn't wanna press charges because I wanted
    to move on
6 months has gone by ... people are posting pics of bleach,
    Clorex and ditches.
tagging me ... I was doing a lot better too ... They said
She should try a different bleach. I hope she dies this time and
    isn't so stupid.
They said I hope she sees this and kills herself ...

Why do I get this? I messed up but why follow me.
I left your guys city ... Im constanty crying now ...
Everyday I think why am I still here?
My anxiety is horrible now. never went out this summer
All from my past ... lifes never getting better ... cant go to school
meet or be with people ... contstanly cutting. Im really depressed
Im on anti deppresants now and councelling and a month ago
   this summer
I overdosed ... In hospital for 2 days ...
Im stuck ... whats left of me now ... nothing stops
I have nobody ... I need someone [sad face]
my name is Amanda Todd ...[1]

Amanda Todd, a fifteen-year-old student from British Columbia, Canada, posted this haunting video of herself to YouTube on September 7, 2012. Just over a month later, on October 10, 2012, she committed suicide.[2]

In the months following her death, Amanda Todd's story gained widespread attention through both the news media and social networks. Her experience brought even greater attention to the issue of cyberbullying, which the National Crime Prevention Council defines as the use of the Internet, cell phones, or other electronic devices to send or post text or images intended to hurt or embarrass another person. Cyberbullying can include spreading lies or rumors about someone online, posting pictures of victims without their consent, or sending mean or abusive text messages.[3] Studies by the Cyberbullying Research Center suggest that between 20-30 percent of teens have been cyberbullied at some time in their lives.[4]

In many ways, cyberbullying is very similar to traditional face-to-face bullying in both its forms and its effects. But the anonymity and lack of supervision of the Internet makes it possible for bullies to engage in their tactics without having to face their victims. And the constant connectedness of teens through the Internet and cell phones makes it difficult for victims to escape their tormentors.[5]

To minimize the danger of being cyberbullied, it is important to remember a few important rules:

• The Internet never forgets—once a word or a picture leaves your computer or cell phone, you lose control of it forever. Messages can be forwarded, photos can be downloaded and saved. Never say or post anything online that you would not want posted on the walls of your school.

• Never post or share personal information (address, phone number, or any information that would make it possible for a stranger to find you) online.

• Always be wary of anyone you meet online, and especially anyone who pushes you to meet in person.

• Don't pass along messages about someone else that you think aren't right, and block users who bully others.

Most importantly, just as with other bullies, don't be afraid to tell a parent or teacher what has happened to you.[6]

Chapter Notes

Chapter 1. One Teen's Story

1. All quotes from a telephone interview with "Chandra," November 30, 2003.

Chapter 2. Bullying: What Is It? Who Does It?

1. Herbert Lindgren, "Bullying—How to Stop It!" *NebFacts*, Nebraska Cooperative Extension NF96-309, n.d., <http://www.ianr.unl.edu/pubs/family/nf309.htm> (September 12, 2002).

2. Peter Sheras, PhD, *Your Child: Bully or Victim? Understanding and Ending School Yard Tyranny* (New York: Fireside, 2002), p. 25.

3. Debra Viadero, "Bullies Beware," *Education Week*, May 28, 1997, pp. 19–21.

4. "Survey Finds Bullying Widespread in Schools," *Mental Health Weekly*, May 14, 2001, <http://www.findarticles.com/cf_O/mOB-SC/19_11.../article.jhtml?term=bullies%2C=bullying> (August 26, 2003).

5. "New Survey Finds Alarming Increase of Bullying . . . Secret to Self-Esteem Program Addresses Timely Issues Confronting Teen Girls and Boys," *Business Wire*, February 6, 2002, <http://www.find-articles.com/cf_O/mOEIN/2002_Feb_6/82582014/print.jhtml> (August 26, 2003).

6. Lindgren.

7. Sue Smith-Heavenrich, "Kids Hurting Kids: Bullies in the Schoolyard," *Mothering*, May–June 2001, <http://www.findarticles.com/cf_0/m0838/20...ne/76587491/p1/article.jhtml?term=bullies> (August 25, 2003).

8. Brooke Donald, "As Crime Falls, Students Still Afraid," *The Star-Ledger*, December 10, 2002, p. 45.

9. Sheras, p. 22.

10. Ibid., p. 25.

11. Ibid., p. 27.

12. Hara Estroff Marano, "Big. Bad. Bully." *Psychology Today*, September–October, 1995, p. 54.

13. Sheras, p. 28.

14. Ibid., p. 28.

15. Marano, p. 56.

16. Ibid., p. 56.

Chapter 3. **Why Do Bullies Do It and Why Do Victims Take It?**

1. Peter Sheras, PhD, *Your Child: Bully or Victim? Understanding and Ending School Yard Tyranny* (New York: Fireside, 2002), pp. 25–26.

2. John Dayton Cerna, "Bully and Victim No More," *Advocate Commentary: The National Gay & Lesbian Newsmagazine Internet Site*, n.d., <http://www.advocate.com/html/stories/835/835_bullies.asp> (September 12, 2002).

3. Telephone interview with Bruce Nerenberg, PhD, February 17, 2003.

4. Ibid.

5. Quoted in Hara Estroff Marano, "Big. Bad. Bully." *Psychology Today*, September–October, 1995, p. 54.

6. David Johnson and Geraldine Lewis, "Do You Like What You See? Self-Perceptions of Adolescent Bullies," *British Educational Research Journal*, vol. 25, issue 5, December 1999, <http://www.web18.epnet.com/citation.asp?tb=1&...+sm+KS+so+b+ss+SO+9CA2&cf=1&fn=101&m=105> (September 16, 2002).

7. Nerenberg.

8. Marano, p. 54.

9. Ibid.

10. Nerenberg.

11. Personal interview with Marilyn LaCourt, family therapist, January 14, 2003.

12. Ibid.

13. "Bullies See More of TV Violence, Less of Adults," *Brown University Child & Adolescent Behavior Letter*, vol.12, issue 10, October 1996, <http://www.web18.epnet.com/citation.asp?tb=1&...+sm+KS+so+b+ss+SO+9CA2&cf=1&fn=171&m=174> (September 16, 2002).

14. Stuart Teplin et al., "Parental Maltreatment and Emotional Dysregulation as Risk Factors for Bullying and Victimization in Middle Childhood," *Journal of Developmental & Behavioral Pediatrics*, February 2002, <http://www.findarticles.com/cf_O/mOHVD/1_pl/article.jhtml?term=bullies%2C=bullying> (August 26, 2003).

15. Ron Banks, "Bullying in Schools," *ERIC, Clearing House on Elementary and Childhood Education*, March 1997 <http://ericeece.org/pubs/digest/ 1997/banks97.html> (September 19, 2002).

16. Sheras, pp. 19–20.

17. Ibid., p. 76.

18. "Bullying Common, Linked to Poor Psychosocial Adjustment," *Brown University Child and Adolescent Behavior Letter*, June 2001, <http://www.findarticles.com/cf_O/mO537/6_...pl/article.jhtml?term=bullies%2C=bullying> (August 26, 2003); and Banks.

19. Sheras, pp. 75–76.

20. Telephone interview with Connie Emmons, M.S., May 13, 2003.

21. Telephone interview with "Randi," August 8, 2003.

22. Judith Bernstein et al., "Children Who Are Targets of Bullying," *Journal of Interpersonal Violence*, vol. 12, issue 4, August 1997, <http://web18.epnet.com/citation.asp?tb=1&...+sm+KS+so+b+ss+SO+9CA2&cf=1&fn=151&m=155> (September 16, 2002).

23. Nerenberg.

24. Beverly Yahnke, PhD, "What Makes A Kid's Clique Tick?" 2003.

25. Nerenberg.

26. Linda Voss and Jean Mulligan, "Bullying in School: Are Short Pupils at Risk?" *British Medical Journal*, n.d., <http://www.findarticles.com/cf_0/ m0999/72...pl/article. jhtml?term=bullies%2C+bullying> (August 26, 2003).

27. Lindsey Tanner, "A Heavy Burden," *The Milwaukee Journal–Sentinel*, May 17, 2004, p. 4G.

28. "Schoolwide Prevention of Bullying," *Northwest Regional Educational Laboratory*, December 2001, <http://ericcass.uncg.edu/ virtuallib/bullying/1070.html> (September 12, 2002).

29. Marano, p. 56.

30. Rhee Gold, "Confessions of a Boy Dancer: Running a Gauntlet of Bullying and Name-Calling," *Dance Magazine*, November 2001, <http:// www.findarticles.com/cf_0/m1083/11_75/80116503/ print.jhtml> (August 26, 2002).

31. "2011 National School Climate Survey: LGBT Youth Face Pervasive, But Decreasing Levels of Harassment" *Gay, Lesbian & Straight Education Network*, September 2012, <http://www.glsen.org/ cgi-bin/iowa/all/news/record/2897.html> (December 7, 2012).

32. Telephone interview with "Randi," August 8, 2003.

Chapter 4.   How Bullying Affects Both Bullies and Victims

1. Jodee Blanco, *Please Stop Laughing at Me . . .* (Avon, Mass.: Adams Media Corporation, 2003), pp. 163–164.

2. "Annie's Mailbox" advice column, *The Charlotte Herald-Tribune*, April 12, 2003, p. 4E.

3. Entire list adapted from William Voors, "Bullying," *Paradigm*, Winter 2003, vol. 6, no. 4, pp. 16–17. Added information on points within the list cited individually.

4. Mosby's Medical, *Nursing and Allied Health Dictionary* (St. Louis: C.V. Mosby Company, 2002), p. 501.

5. Peter Sheras, PhD, *Your Child: Bully or Victim? Understanding and Ending School Yard Tyranny* (New York: Fireside, 2002), p. 59.

6. Rittakerttu Kaltiala-Heno et al., "Bullying, depression and suicidal ideation in Finnish adolescents," *British Medical Journal*, vol. 391, August 7, 1999, <http://www.findarticles.com/cf_O/m0999/72...19/55552956/pl/article.jhtml?term_bullies> (August 25, 2003).

7. Darcia Harris Bowman, "At School, a Cruel Culture," *Education Week*, March 21, 2001, <http://www.edweek.org/ew/ewstory/cfm?slug=27 taunts.h20> (September 12, 2002).

8. Telephone interview with Bruce Nerenberg, PhD, February 17, 2003.

9. Personal interview with "Phil," August 6, 2003.

10. Blanco, pp. 2–3, 256–257.

11. Hara Estroff Marano, "Big. Bad. Bully." *Psychology Today*, September–October, 1995, p. 56.

12. Dan Olweus, PhD, quoted in Marano, p. 56.

13. Carol Tritt and Renae Duncan, "The Relationship Between Childhood Bullying and Young Adult Self-Esteem and Loneliness," *Journal of Humanistic Education and Development*, September 1997, vol. 36, issue 1, <http://www.web18.epnet.com/citation.asp?tb=sm+KS+so+b+ss+SO+9CA2&cf=1&fn=151&m=152> (September 16, 2002).

14. Marano, p. 68.

15. Ibid., p. 54.

16. Melissa DeRosier, PhD, University of North Carolina, cited in Marano, p. 54.

17. Sheras, p. 74.

18. Ibid.

19. Marano, p. 52.

20. Ibid., p. 68.

21. Marano, p. 69.

22. Leonard Eron, quoted in Bob Ehlert, "Beating Back the Bully," *Better Homes and Gardens*, April 2000, <http://www.findarticles.com/cf_0/m1041/4_78/61184801/pl/article.jhtml?term=bullies> (August 25, 2003).

23. Richard Tremblay, PhD, quoted in Marano, p. 70.

24. Kaltiala-Heno et al.

25. Ibid.

26. Blanco, p. 270.

Chapter 5.   When Girls Bully

1. Telephone interview with Alex, August 26, 2003.

2. Rachel Simmons, *Odd Girl Out: the Hidden Culture of Aggression in Girls* (New York: Harcourt, Inc., 2002), p. 3.

3. Rosalind Wiseman, *Queen Bees and Wannabes: Helping Your Daughter Survive Cliques, Gossip, Boyfriends, and Other Realities of Adolescence* (New York: Three Rivers Press, 2002), pp. 25–35.

4. Simmons, pp. 79–80.

5. Ibid., p. 80.

6. Ibid., pp. 87, 88.

7. Shannon Casey-Cannon, Chris Hayward, and Kris Gowen, "Middle-School Girls' Reports of Peer Victimization: Concerns, Consequences, and Implications," *Professional School Counseling*, vol. 5, issue 2, December 2001, <http://web9.epnet.com/citation.asp?tb=1&_...91+sm+KS+so+b+ss+SO+C1FD&cf=1&fn=81&m=85> (September 13, 2002).

8. Simmons, pp. 156–157.

9. Kathleen O'Brien, "How to Survive the Early Teen Years," *The Star-Ledger*, July 28, 2002, p. 2.

10. Ibid.

11. Ibid., p. 1.

12. Wiseman, pp. 197–199.

13. Marion Underwood, PhD, quoted in Margaret Talbot, "Girls Just Want to be Mean," *The New York Times*, February 24, 2002, p. 24 ff.

14. Wiseman, p. 77.

15. Ibid., p. 10.

16. Ibid., p. 128.

17. Ibid., p. 131.

18. Emily White, *Fast Girls: Teenage Tribes and the Myth of the Slut* (New York: Berkeley Books, 2002), pp. 117–118.

19. Telephone interview with Mary Irish, M.A., August 5, 2003.

20. Adapted from Wiseman, pp. 139–141.

21. Patrick Welsh, "Bully-Boy Focus Overlooks Vicious Acts by Girls," *USA Today*, June 12, 2001, p. 15A.

22. Ibid.

Chapter 6. Anti-Bullying Programs at School

1. Anne Davis, "Fearing Rise in Bullying, Schools Step Up Efforts to Empower Students," *The Milwaukee Journal-Sentinel*, January 27, 2004, p. 1B.

2. Rosalind Wiseman, *Queen Bees and Wannabes: Helping Your Daughter Survive Cliques, Gossip, Boyfriends and Other Realities of Adolescence* (New York: Three Rivers Press, 2002), p. 199.

3. Peter Sheras, PhD, *Your Child: Bully or Victim? Understanding and Ending School Yard Tyranny* (New York: Fireside, 2002), p. 64.

4. Nan Stein, Teacher magazine, August/September 1997, quoted in Colleen Newquist, "Bully-Proof Your School," *Education*

World, Best of '97 Issue, <http://www.education-world.com/a_admin /admin018.shtml> (September 12, 2002).

5. Dan Olweus, *Bullying at School: What We Know and What We Can Do* (Oxford UK and Cambridge USA: Blackwell, 1993, revised 2000), p. 20.

6. Bully Police USA, <http://www.bullypolice.org> (December 14, 2012).

7. Sharon Cromwell, "Stop Bullying Before It Starts!" *Education World*, June 7, 1999, <http://www.educationworld.com/a_admin/ admin117.shtml> (September 12, 2002).

8. Olweus, p. 69.

9. Ibid., p. 25.

10. Adapted from Ibid., p. 82.

11. Adapted from Ibid., pp. 84–85.

12. Personal interview with Michael Bralick and Marianne Kirsh, January 30, 2003.

13. Ibid.

14. Ibid.

15. Ibid.

16. Personal "Round Table" interview with Debbie Stears, Pat Haislmaier, Susan McDonald, Ceil Carse, and Gina Nau, February 13, 2003.

17. Ibid.

18. Ibid.

19. Ibid.

20. Ibid.

21. Ibid.

22. Bralick and Kirsh.

23. Olweus, pp. 113–114.

24. Allan Beane, PhD, *The Bully Free Classroom: Over 100 Tips*

and Strategies for Teachers K–8 (Minneapolis: Free Spirit Publishing, 1999), pp. 59, 61.

Chapter 7.   Dealing With a Bully

1. Personal interview with Gary, September 6, 2003.

2. Hara Estroff Marano, "Big. Bad. Bully." *Psychology Today,* September–October, 1995, p. 55.

3. Personal interview with Marilyn LaCourt, family therapist, January 4, 2003.

4. Lisa Walls, "Bullying and Sexual Harassment in Schools," *Committee for Children*, n.d., <http://www.cfchildren.org/PU bully.html> (September 12, 2002).

5. Adapted from "Bullying—A Few Suggestions from Educate Online," n.d., <http://www.educate.co.uk/bullsug.htm> (September 12, 2002).

6. "Dealing With Bullying: Standing Up for Yourself—or a Friend," *TeensHealth*, n.d., <http://kidshealth.org/teen/your_mind/problems/bullies_p4.html> (September 19, 2002).

7. Telephone interview with David, February 11, 2003.

8. Myrna Shure, "Bullies and Their Victims: A Problem-Solving Approach to Prevention," *The Brown University Child and Adolescent Behavior Letter*, October 2000, <http://www.findarticles.com/cf_0/m0537/10_16/67325679/pl/article.jhtml?term=bullies> (August 25, 2003).

9. "Bullying—A Few Suggestions from Educate Online."

10. E-mail interview with Marcus, August 6, 2003.

11. Rosalind Wiseman, *Queen Bees and Wannabes: Helping Your Daughter Survive Cliques, Gossip, Boyfriends, and Other Realities of Adolescence* (New York: Three Rivers Press, 2002), p. 199.

12. "New Survey Finds Alarming Increase of Bullying Among Girls; Secret to Self-Esteem Programs Addresses Timely

Issues Confronting Teen Girls and Boys," *Business Wire*, February 6, 2002, <http://www.findarticles.com/cf_0/m0EIN/2002_Feb_6/82582012/print.jhtml> (August 26, 2003).

13. Telephone interview with Marcus, August 6, 2003.

14. Telephone interview with Jessie, February 2, 2004.

15. Telephone interview with David, February 11, 2003.

16. Ibid.

17. Telephone interview with Jessie, February 2, 2004.

18. Peter Sheras, PhD, *Your Child: Bully or Victim?—Understanding and Ending School Yard Tyranny* (New York: Fireside, 2002), p. 99.

19. Ibid.

20. Adapted from Ibid., pp. 98–99.

21. Ibid., p. 186.

22. Ibid., p. 187.

23. Ibid., pp. 130–132.

Chapter 8   Cyberbullying

1. Amanda Todd, transcript of video "My story: Stuggling, bullying, suicide, self harm," September 7, 2012, <http://www.youtube.com/watch?v=vOHXGNx-E7E> (January 18, 2013).

2. Gillian Shaw and Lori Culbert, "Port Coquitlam teen driven to death by cyberbullying," *Vancouver Sun*, October 12, 2012, <http://www.vancouversun.com/technology/Port+Coquitlam+teen+driven+death+cyberbullying+with+video/7375941/story.html#ixzz2Jb9IAaWk> (January 18, 2013).

3. Cyberbullying–National Crime Prevention Council, <http://www.ncpc.org/cyberbullying> (January 21, 2013).

4. Summary of Cyberbullying Research 2004–2010—Cyberbullying Research Center, <http://www.cyberbullying.us/research.php> (January 21, 2013).

5. Justin W. Patchin and Sameer Hinduja, "Bullies Move Beyond the Schoolyard: A Preliminary Look at Cyberbullying," *Youth Violence and Juvenile Justice*, 2006 <http://yvj.sagepub.com/content/4/2/148.full.pdf+html> (January 21, 2013).

6. Cyberbullying–National Crime Prevention Council, <http://www.ncpc.org/cyberbullying> (January 31, 2013).

Glossary

abuse (noun)—Actions that are done to hurt another person in various ways.

abuse (verb)—To harm someone else, mentally, emotionally, sexually, or physically.

aggression—An action intended to harm someone else. A person doing so would be described as aggressive.

alliance—A group that bands together and works for the benefit of the whole group. In the bullying context, a group that supports each other while excluding or hurting others.

antisocial—Being filled with anger, not understanding the difference between right and wrong, and harming others.

bully (noun)—A person who uses ongoing physical or verbal mistreatment to do harm to another person, usually, but not always, someone smaller or weaker in some way.

bully (verb)—To use ongoing physical or verbal mistreatment to do harm to another person, usually, but not always, someone smaller or weaker in some way.

clique—A group of friends who "hang out" together and may exclude others.

conflict resolution—To come to an agreement about something people are fighting about.

defiance—Refusal to obey rules or people in authority.

depression—A mental state in which a person is sad and feels hopeless and worthless in a way that is out of proportion to reality.

emotional abuse—To harm someone emotionally by attacking, taunting, or otherwise mistreating him or her.

empathy—The ability to understand what someone else is feeling.

exclusion, excluding—Keeping someone out of a group.

homosexuality—Being sexually attracted to people of the same sex instead of the opposite sex. Men who are attracted to other men are usually called gay; women attracted to other women are usually called lesbians, although they can also be called gay.

internalize—To take someone else's opinion of you and make it your own.

isolate—To make someone be entirely alone, outside the group.

passive—To not stand up for oneself; to allow someone else to direct what one does.

pecking order—A slang term for how people fit in the social structure, from those on top down to those on the bottom.

peer mediation—Solving a conflict by having a peer mediator listen to both sides and guide the parties to a win-win solution.

popular—Liked by others.

rage—Extreme anger.

relational aggression—A term for the type of bullying girls often do by excluding someone, spreading rumors, or telling lies.

reputation—What others think of a person.

reciprocity—A term for giving something back that is the same as what one has received.

restraining order—A legal order, issued by a court, which tells someone to leave someone else alone. It may put limits on how close the person may come to his victim.

revenge—The act of getting back at someone who has wronged another.

rumor—Something that is not necessarily true said about some-one.

self-esteem—How a person feels about him- or herself.

slut—Someone, usually a woman, with low sexual morals. The word is often used by teenagers to insult someone.

social scientists—People who study human behavior.

social skills—The ability to get along with people, to make and keep friends.

submissiveness—Doing what another person wants you to do, even if it is not in your best interest.

survey—A tool used by social scientists to learn about human behavior. People answer questions on paper, in person, or on the telephone, which the researchers use to create a score.

teasing—To make fun of someone. Sometimes it is gentle and done in fun. Sometimes it is cruel and meant to hurt someone.

taunting—A more severe form of teasing.

victim—In the context of bullying, someone who is on the receiving end of the mistreatment.

For More Information

KidsPeace National Center for Kids Overcoming Crisis
1–800–334–4543

National Resource Center for Safe Schools
1–800–268–2275

National Suicide Prevention Hotline
1–800–SUICIDE

National Mental Health Association (NMHA)
1–800–696–6642

Further Reading

Blanco, Jodee. *Please Stop Laughing at Me*. Avon, Mass.: Adams Media, 2003.

Golus, Carrie. *Take a Stand!: What You Can Do About Bullying*. Minneapolis, Minn.: Lerner Publications Co., 2009.

Hunter, Nick. *Cyber Bullying*. Chicago: Heinemann Library, 2012.

Karres, Erika V. Shearin. *Mean Chicks, Cliques, and Dirty Tricks: A Real Girl's Guide to Getting Through the Day with Smarts and Style*. Avon, Mass.: Adams Media, 2004.

Kuykendall, Sally. *Bullying*. Santa Barbara, Calif.: Greenwood, 2012.

Peterson, Judy Monroe. *How to Beat Cyberbullying*. New York: Rosen Central, 2013.

Shapiro, Ouisie. *Bullying and Me: Schoolyard Stories*. Chicago: Albert Whitman & Company, 2010.

Simmons, Rachel. *Odd Girl Speaks Out: Girls Write About Bullies, Cliques, Popularity and Jealousy*. Orlando: Harcourt, 2004.

Internet Addresses

Bullying.org

<http://www.bullying.org>

Stop Bullying Now!

<http://www.stopbullyingnow.com>

KidsHealth

<http://www.kidshealth.org>

Index